Henry Cole and the Chamber of Horrors

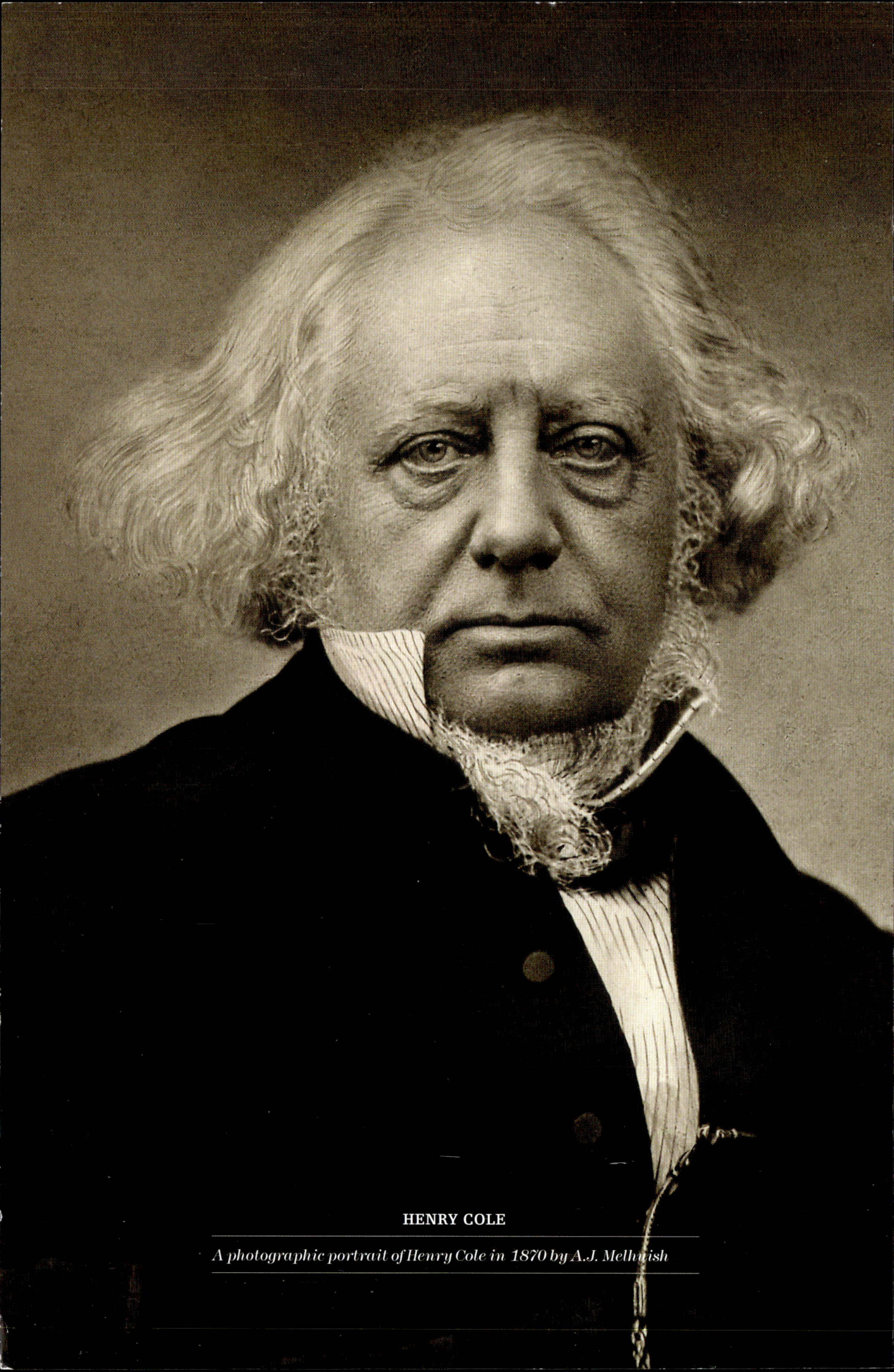

HENRY COLE

A photographic portrait of Henry Cole in 1870 by A.J. Melhuish

HENRY COLE AND THE CHAMBER OF HORRORS

THE CURIOUS ORIGINS OF THE VICTORIA AND ALBERT MUSEUM

Being the first 'Henry Cole Lecture' given
on 30 October 2008, at the Sackler Centre, V&A

CHRISTOPHER
FRAYLING

V&A Publishing

Being the first 'Henry Cole Lecture'
given on 30 October 2008 at the Sackler Centre, V&A

First published by V&A Publishing, 2010

V&A Publishing
Victoria and Albert Museum
South Kensington
London SW7 2RL

Paperback edition

ISBN 978 1 85177 623 8

10 9 8 7 6 5 4 3 2 1
2014 2013 2012 2011 2010

A catalogue record for this book is available from the British Library.

Design direction: *David Pocknell*
Designer: *Harry Pocknell*
Editor: *Roger Sears*

Printed in Italy

V&A Publishing
Victoria and Albert Museum
South Kensington
London SW7 2RL
www.vandabooks.com

'When we want steam, we must get Cole.'

attributed to Prince Albert by his daughter, the Princess Royal

Foreword 7
By Mark Jones

Two Terriers 9
In which we meet Jim and his energetic master Henry Cole, and learn something about their unfortunate experiences of education.

The Government Officer 17
In which we visit a joyless classroom in Charles Dickens's Coketown, in distinguished company, and see a glimmer of hope.

A Museum of Ornamental Art 23
In which Henry Cole persuades friends in high places to let him move the School of Design to Marlborough House, and open a new kind of Museum there too.

A House Full of Horrors 27
In which visitors to the Museum are exposed, before anything else, to some nightmares of bad design .

Indefensible in Principle 33
In which we are taken, catalogue in hand, on a guided tour of the Chamber of Horrors, with full explanations provided.

The Etruscan Tea Set 57
In which we learn at last about Henry Cole's own taste in design, and discover that it is not as easy as he thought to tell the difference.

A Powerful Antidote to the Gin Palace 73
In which the Museum of Manufactures evolves, through curatorial selection and the survival of the fittest, into the great Victoria and Albert Museum.

Head, Heart & Hand 83
In which John Ruskin helps us through the subsequent story of art and design education in South Kensington and beyond, and we are reunited with Jim.

List of Illustrations 94

Notes 96

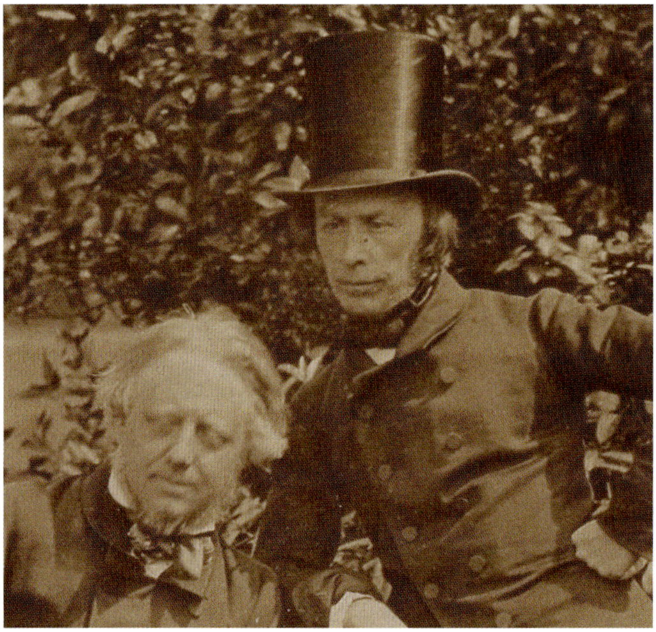

A DESIGN PARTNERSHIP

Cole photographed with Richard Redgrave in the gardens of Gore House, probably in the 1860s

Opening in the wake of the 1851 Great Exhibition the V&A (then known as the South Kensington Museum) had, from its foundation, a unique mission – the education of designers in the principles of design, of the public as consumers of design, and of young people as the designers and consumers of the future.

Henry Cole, the Museum's first Director, was joint head of the Government Department of Science and Art. At his initiative, the department developed a national touring exhibition programme, supported the creation of museums in Dublin and Edinburgh, and provided new schools of science and schools of art with scientific equipment and casts of some of the finest sculpture in Europe. The South Kensington System, as it became known, transformed the landscape of educational opportunities in Britain and was widely imitated abroad. Its influence is still felt today.

The moving force behind all these developments in South Kensington was the Royal Commission for the Exhibition of 1851. Established initially under the chairmanship of Prince Albert to organise and stage the Great Exhibition, the first ever World Fair, it applied the substantial profit made from that enterprise to purchase 87 acres of land in South Kensington. It helped establish the area's three great museums, the Royal Albert Hall and renowned institutions of learning, including Imperial College and the Royal Colleges of Art and Music. South Kensington became and remains the world's greatest public intellectual resource in the arts and sciences. When this huge undertaking was complete, sufficient funds remained for the Royal Commission to set up, in 1891, an educational trust to perpetuate its aims. The 1851 Royal Commission continues this work to this day.

In 2008 the V&A reaffirmed its commitment to its educational mission by opening the Sackler Centre for arts education. On 30 October 2008, to celebrate this development, Professor Sir Christopher Frayling gave the inaugural Henry Cole Lecture, which celebrated the legacy of the Museum's founding director.

The lecture in itself was a landmark event. It offers fresh insights on the early history of the Museum, and sets out a challenging agenda for the future of design education in Britain. We are grateful to Sir Christopher for his extraordinary contribution to the development of the Museum, as a trustee from 1984 to 2009, and as an unrivalled interpreter of Henry Cole's work.

We are also grateful to the 1851 Commission for co-funding the publication of the lecture, which has enabled the Museum to distribute it to a far wider audience.

Mark Jones
Director, Victoria and Albert Museum

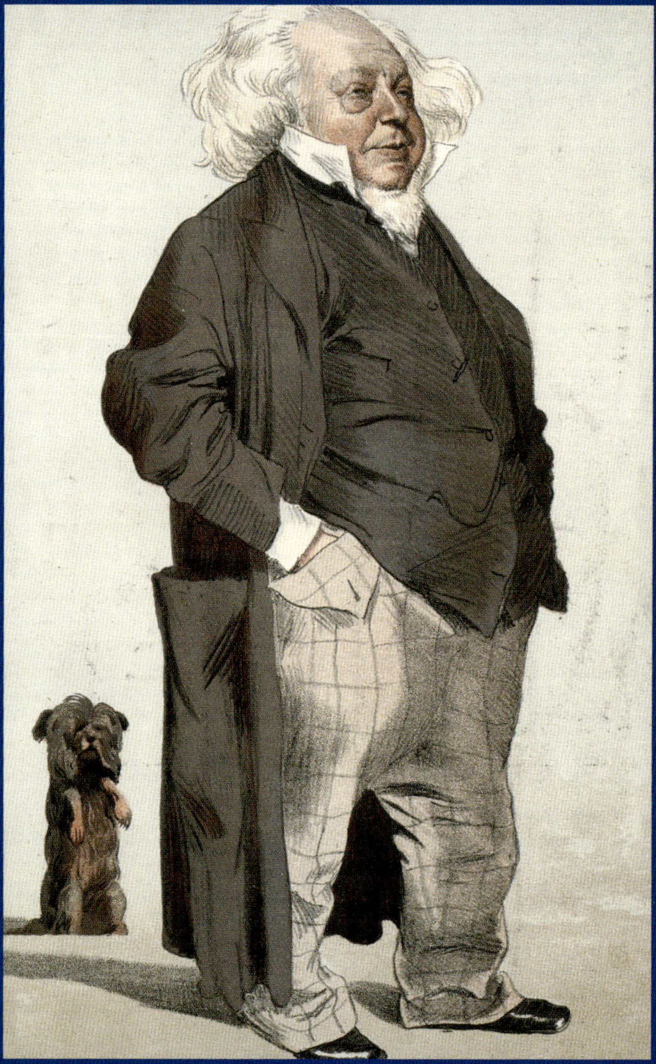

TWO TERRIERS

Caricature of Henry Cole by James Tissot for Vanity Fair, *August 1871*

Two Terriers

In which we meet Jim and his energetic master Henry Cole, and learn something about their unfortunate experiences of education.

Hidden away in the garden of the South Kensington Museum – now the Madejski garden of the V&A – there is a small and easily overlooked commemorative plaque, which does not have a museum number. It reads 'In Memory of Jim, Died 1879, Aged 15 Years. Faithful Dog of Sir Henry Cole, of this Museum'. Jim had in fact died on 30 January 1879. He was with Henry Cole in his heyday, as the King of South Kensington – its museums and colleges – and saw him through to retirement from the public service and beyond. And next to this inscription there's another one dedicated to Jim's successor Tycho and dated 1885. Both dogs are actually buried in the garden.

We know from Henry Cole's voluminous diary that, between 1864 and 1879, Jim, a Cairn terrier, was often to be seen in public at his master's side. An earlier terrier was to be seen at Henry Cole's side in the very same garden in 1861, when he watched the Prince Consort inspecting the new memorial to the Great Exhibition of 1851, now located behind the Albert Hall. It included a statue of Prince Albert by Joseph Durham, on a lofty plinth covered in statistics about the income, expenditure and numbers of visitors to the Great Exhibition: 6,039,195 visitors, to be exact. Cole had been a tireless champion of Prince Albert. According to the Princess Royal – later to become Empress of Prussia – there was a family saying in the Palace at the time, invented by Albert himself, that when things needed doing: 'when we want steam, we must get Cole'. We may therefore assume that as the Prince Consort leaned forward to see the memorial more clearly, Cole was interested in the inscription, the statistics and the likeness of Prince Albert, while the terrier was more interested in the possibilities of the plinth and of the garden.

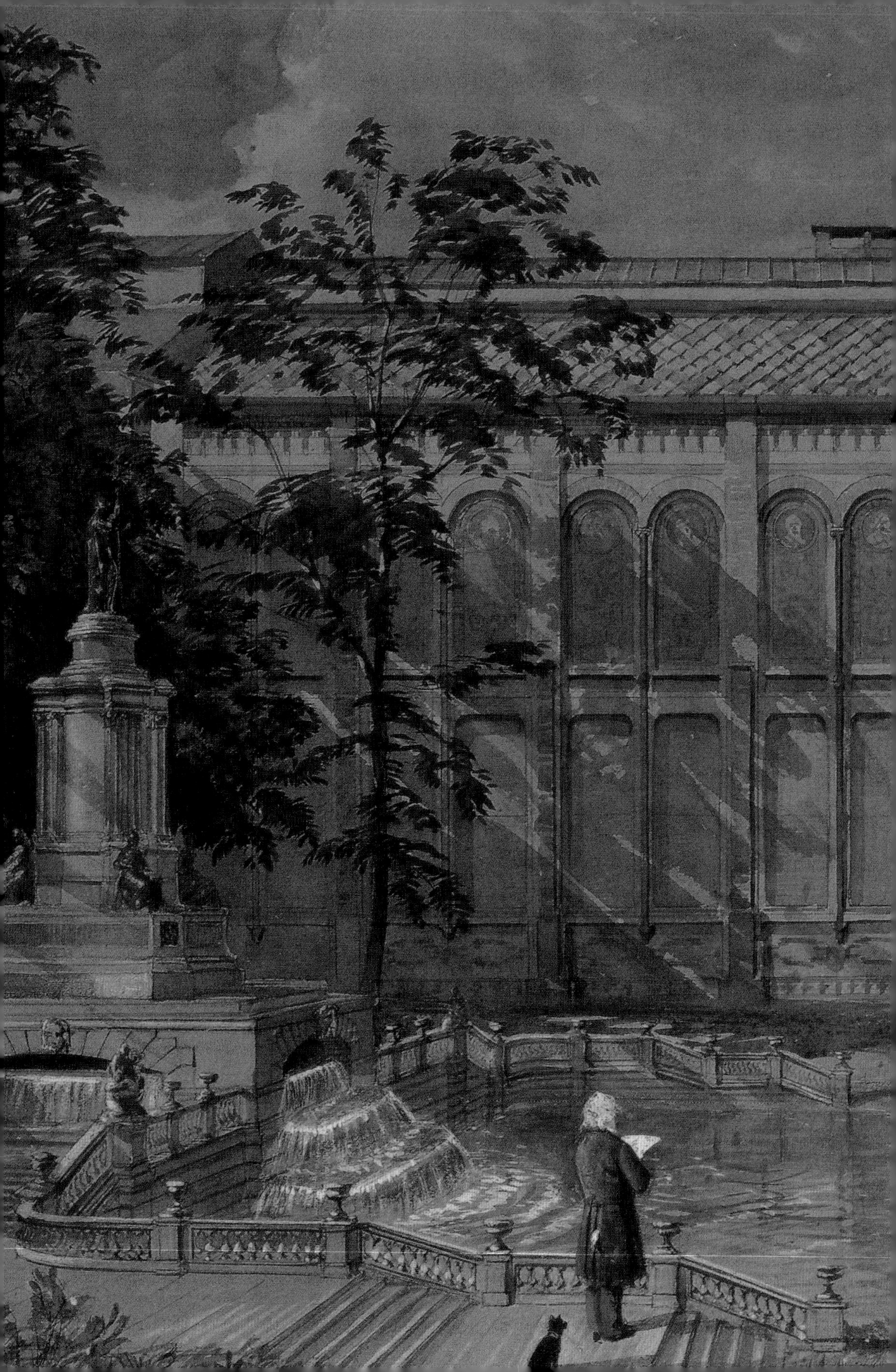

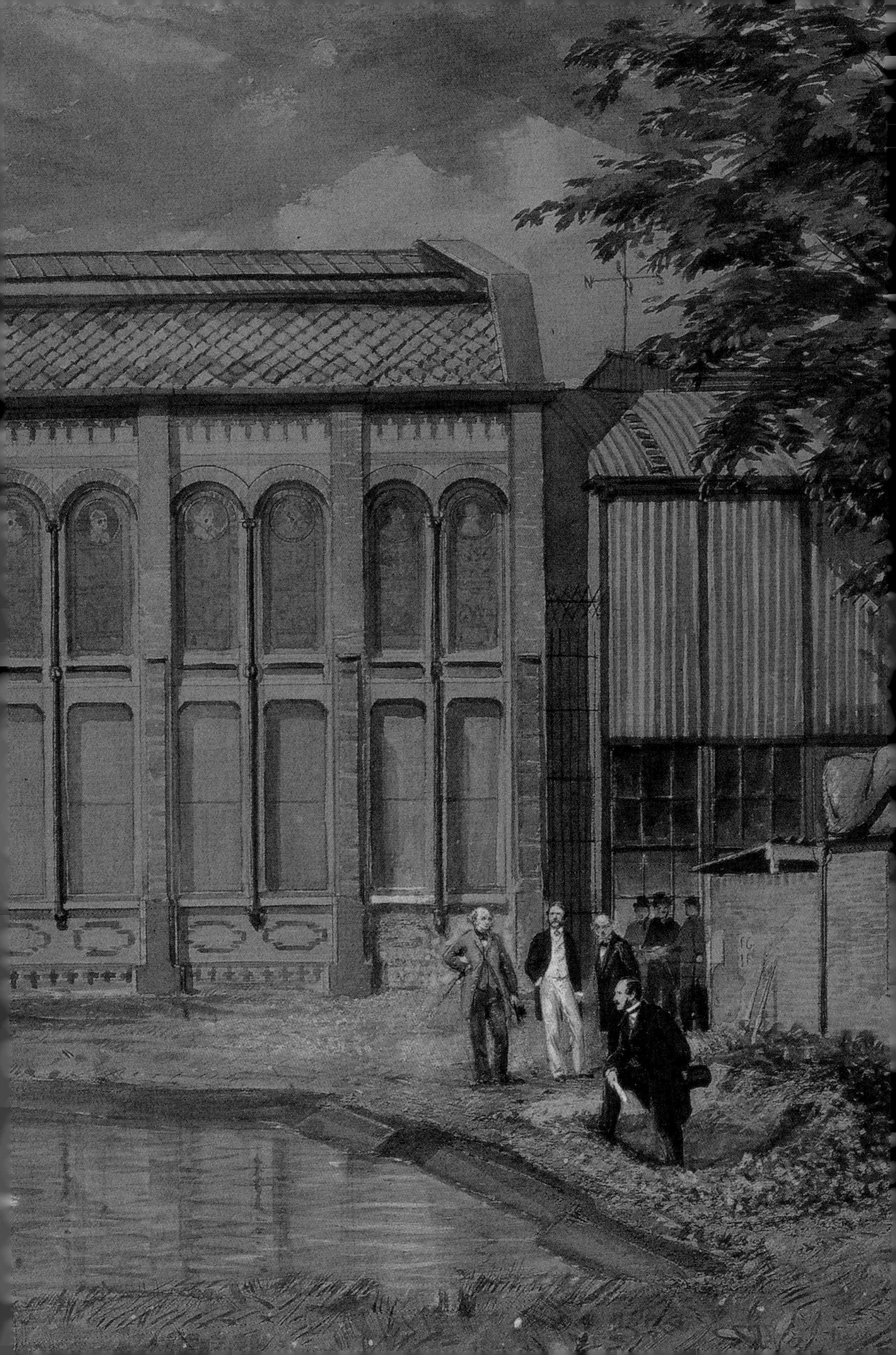

In early 1866, first thing in the morning, soon after the workmen's bell had rung, Henry and Jim would set forth together from Cole's newly constructed official residence in the Museum – where he'd moved in July 1863 – to tour the building sites of South Kensington – a name which it is said was first invented by Cole when he named the museum the South Kensington Museum, to describe the new developments happening around Brompton Church. According to *The Builder* magazine, these two well-known figures would 'be seen clambering over bricks, mortar and girders, up ladders and about scaffolding'. Several buildings, in the South Kensington Renaissance Revival style, were springing up all around them: the Natural History Museum, the College of Science, the extension of this Museum …

Then, from February to November 1867, when the Cole family went to Paris so that Henry could help supervise the British section of the huge Paris Universal Exposition – a stressful experience, which at last cured Henry Cole of the blockbusting international exposition habit, for life – Jim had joined them, in their controversially luxurious residence at No. 21 Champs Elysée, a newly built mansion.

And on the morning the Bethnal Green Museum opened, 24 June 1872, Jim showed a healthy distaste for his master's well-known predilection for pomp and circumstance. Henry Cole had changed into his court suit to join the Royal Procession. As he emerged from his bedroom, on the great day, he found Jim completely poleaxed: 'Seeing me in uniform', wrote Cole, 'he stood motionless at the top of the stairs instead of rushing down [as he did] every morning'. Maybe Jim had got wind of the fact that the lower floors of the Bethnal Green Museum were to be entirely devoted to the 'animal products collection', banished from South Kensington. The collection, which had mainly been gleaned from the Schools of Design or from the 1851 Exhibition, included among the textiles 'a pair of cuffs handspun and knitted from the hair of French poodle dogs'. No wonder Jim stood motionless at the top of the stairs.

The dutiful terrier also accompanied his master on numerous summer holidays to Elm Cottage in the village of Shere – between Guildford and Dorking – where Cole would go and think up yet more schemes and campaigns for South Kensington.

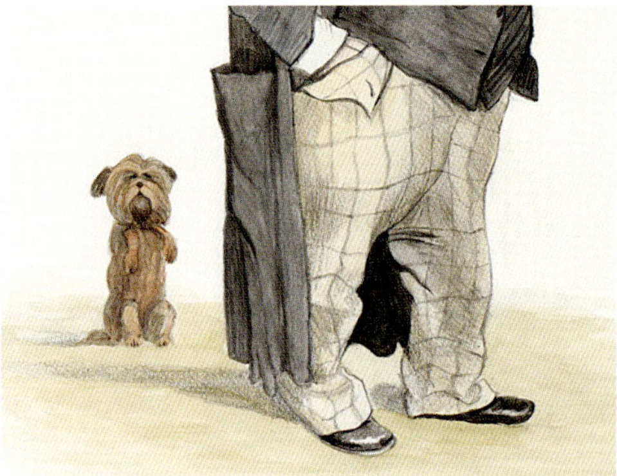

MASTER & DOG

Detail of a watercolour of Cole and Jim by the author, painted for the V&A's 150th anniversary album

So when 'King Cole' was affectionately caricatured by James Tissot for *Vanity Fair* in 1871, the seven-year-old Jim was there at his side. Cole was somewhat vertically challenged – and Jim, sitting on his hind legs, may have been put in for scale. His master was by then well-known about town for his flowing white hair, his whiskers, his frock coat with flapping coat-tails, his bulging waistcoat and baggy trousers. A couple of years ago, Mark Jones, the Director, asked me to contribute an image to the V&A's 150th birthday album – and so it was to this one that I turned. My caption read: 'Henry Cole's faithful and inseparable terrier Jim … was around for much of Chapter One of the V&A's building … Master and dog were both terriers. Jim apparently enjoyed making a great exhibition of himself – and so, of course, did Henry Cole'. Jim was a well-trained and obedient dog, who never disgraced himself or his master in public or private.

The standard and best-selling book on the training of dogs, in Jim's lifetime,

'Master and dog were both terriers. Jim apparently enjoyed making a great exhibition of himself – and so, of course, did Henry Cole.'

was called *Dog Breaking – The most expeditious, certain and easy method whether great excellence or only mediocrity be required* and it was written by one Col. W. N. Hutchinson, late of the Grenadier Guards.[2] It had originally been published by John Murray in 1848 – around the time Cole had his first thoughts about a Great Exhibition – with regular new or revised editions appearing right up to the turn of the century. The point of the book was to persuade dog-owners to abandon the harsh methods of dog breaking – the whip, the spiked collar, the bellowing voice – in favour of constant encouragement, an understanding of the dogs' 'different tempers and dispositions' and the use of easily recognised words, signals and whistles. Col. Hutchinson explicitly made the analogy with human forms of education, from the most basic forms to 'the future double-first collegian'. 'They begin and proceed on the same principle … Believe me, the perfection I have described can never be attained with great severity or flogging.' The redoubtable Colonel was here denying the famous distinction later to be made, according to legend, anyway, by William Morris between education and training: education, said Morris, was what you did with human beings; training was what you did with dogs.

Henry Cole knew, for himself, a thing or two about flogging, from first-hand experience. Here he is, describing some experiences he had at Christ's Hospital School near the City of London, where he was educated from age eight onwards in 1819–23, and where he had – as he later wrote – 'a rather unhappy time of it'. That was putting it mildly. Christ's Hospital at the time – and it was the time of *Tom Brown's Schooldays* – was notorious even among public schools for its harsh regime of corporal punishment. The headmaster was the Rev. Dr Arthur Trollope, a well-furnished and short-fused classical scholar and churchman:

'Half our parrot knowledge was frightened out of us by his impatient

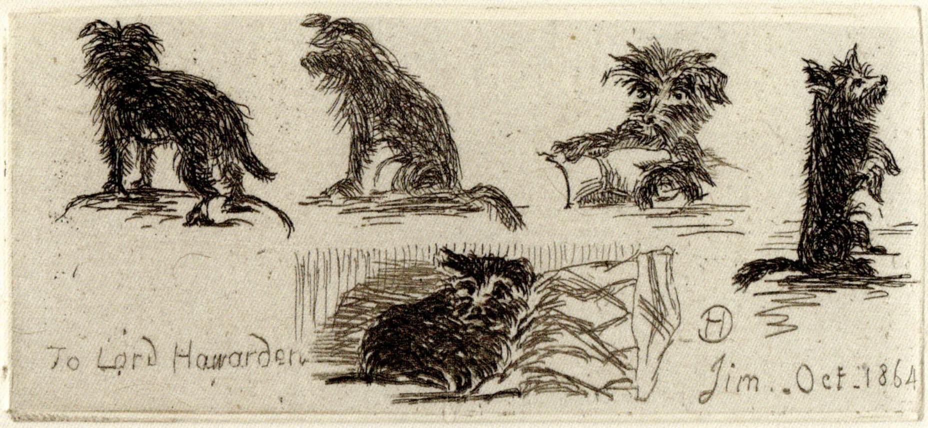

Jim

An etching of the young terrier Jim sketched while at Broadstairs by Henry Cole, dated October 1864, and dedicated to Lord Hawarden

knock at the School door, and then his fussy entrance. … in the morning at the slightest trip, he would thrust his hands into his breeches pockets hastily groping for his keys – unlock the desk in a bungling way, which increased his ire, and seizing a cane he would rush at the head of the boy before he called for the palm of his hand. We all dreaded him and hated the sight of him. He was like an ogre always thirsting for the blood of little boys. I don't remember his ever giving one a word of encouragement. He gave me once the longest and most ferocious caning any boy had from him in my days'.

No wonder the result was what Cole called parrot knowledge. 'I recollect a Latin Grammar written in Latin being put into my hands and being told I was to learn it. By dint of ceaseless gabbling over the words, I got the sounds more or less by heart and could repeat them. But as for the meaning of the words themselves or the sense they conveyed, I had not the dimmest glimmering.'

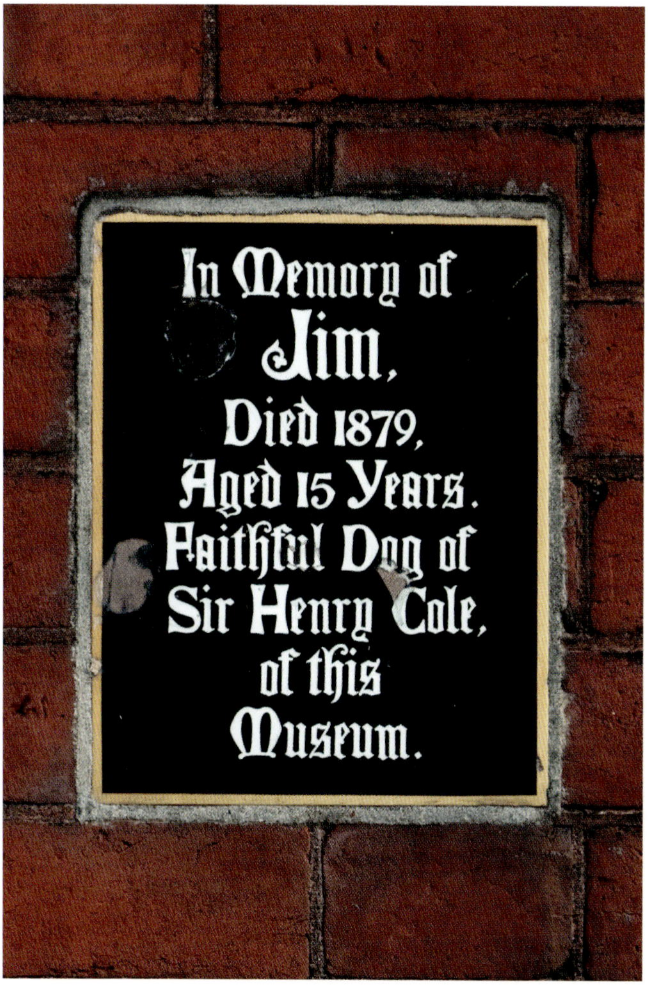

IN MEMORIAM

Memorial plaque 'In Memory of Jim', in the Madejski Garden of the V&A

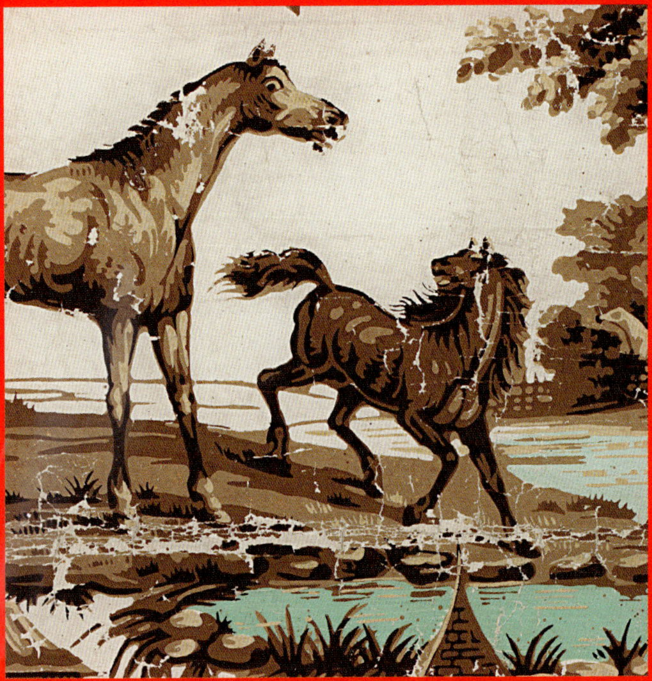

'WOULD YOU PAPER A ROOM?'

Detail of a wallpaper featuring horses, Exhibit 35 in the 'Chamber of Horrors'

The Government Officer

In which we visit a joyless classroom in Charles Dickens's Coketown, in distinguished company, and see a glimmer of hope.

The classroom atmosphere that had been experienced by Cole was immortalised several times by Cole's near-contemporary Charles Dickens – who came from a similar family background, and whose path would often cross or parallel Cole's during the course of his public career.[3] In the year that Cole invented the first Christmas card – 1843 – with its happy family enjoying the Old English festivities, surrounded by examples of charitable good works, Dickens published *A Christmas Carol*, with a very similar final scene. But Cole had also helped to invent the adhesive stamp which went on the envelope. In 1839, Cole had arranged for his polemical playlet about postal reform and the penny post, another subject which exercised him a lot – with Queen Victoria given all the best lines, of course – to be bound in with the monthly parts of *Nicholas Nickleby*. In 1848, Dickens and Cole served together on a Society of Arts Committee, dealing with the vexed issue of intellectual property and the rights of inventors. Dickens was interested for obvious reasons in pirated novels, Cole in design and invention, and Dickens subsequently wrote a fictionalised version of Cole's pamphlet on the subject (which he'd been sent in proof) in his periodical *Household Words* – about an engineer from Birmingham, a smith by trade, who tries with increasing frustration to navigate the expensive and time-consuming 35-stage application process in London to secure a patent. It takes him six weeks and makes him feel as if by 'inventing an ingenious invention meant to do good he [has] done something wrong'. This article anticipated the section of *Little Dorrit* on the Great Circumlocution Office staffed by Tite Barnacles; and it influenced the campaign for the Patent Law Amendment Act. Then, a year or so later, in 1851, Cole and Dickens were to serve together again on a Royal Commission Committee – not a very effective one as it turned out – about working class visitor numbers to the Great Exhibition. Both men were good at using such committees – when they had to – for their own purposes. And they both liked walking with dogs.

But on the one occasion Henry Cole himself was directly satirised in a Dickens novel, he was on the side of the headmaster rather than the boys; on the side of the man who pours children full of imperial gallons of 'useful facts', bare unconnected facts and figures and averages until they are full to the brim with them rather than introducing the children to the world of the imagination, creativity and wonder – which is one of the main themes of the novel. *Hard Times*, Chapter Two, published in *Household Words* as part of the first instalment on 1 April 1854, is called 'Murdering the Innocents'; it is set in the 'bare monotonous vault of a school-room' in industrial Coketown with Mr Gradgrind, the schoolmaster Mr M'Choakumchild and an un-named third gentleman, a 'third grown person' standing at the front of the class. The chapter begins with Sissy Jupe, the uninhibited circus girl – or rather 'girl number twenty' – struggling to give a definition of a horse:

'Girl number twenty unable to define a horse!' said Mr Gradgrind, for the general behoof of all the little pitchers. 'Girl number twenty possessed of no facts, in reference to one of the commonest animals! Some boy's definition of a horse. Bitzer, yours.'

Bitzer is a pale, cold-eyed little boy with short-cropped hair and bad skin. 'Quadruped. Graminivorous. Forty teeth, namely twenty-four grinders, four eye-teeth, and twelve incisive. Sheds coat in spring … Age known by marks in mouth'. This (and much more) Bitzer.

'Now girl number twenty', said Mr Gradgrind, 'You know what a horse is' …

The third gentleman stepped forth.

A mighty man at cutting and drying, he was: a government officer; in his way (and in most other people's too), a professed pugilist; always in training, always with a system to force down the general throat like a bolus, always to be heard of at the bar of his little Public-office, ready to fight all England. He was certain to knock the wind out of common sense, and render that unlucky adversary deaf to the call of time. And he had it in charge from high authority to bring about the great public-office Millennium, when Commissioners should reign upon earth.

'Very well', said this gentleman, briskly smiling, and folding his arms. 'That's a horse. Now, let me ask you girls and boys, Would you paper a room with representations of horses?'

After a pause, one half of the children cried in chorus, 'Yes, sir!' Upon which the other half, seeing in the gentleman's face that Yes was wrong, cried out in chorus, 'No, sir!' – as the custom is, in these examinations.

'Of course, No. Why wouldn't you? ... '

A pause ...

'I'll explain to you, then', said the gentleman, after another and a dismal pause, 'why you wouldn't paper a room with representations of horses. Do you ever see horses walking up and down the sides of rooms in reality – in fact? Do you?'

'Yes, sir!' from one half. 'No, sir!' from the other.

'Of course no', said the gentleman, with an indignant look at the wrong half. 'Why, then, you are not to see anywhere, what you don't see in fact; you are not to have anywhere, what you don't have in fact. What is called Taste, is only another name for Fact.'

Thomas Gradgrind nodded his approbation.

'This is a new principle, a discovery, a great discovery', said the gentleman. 'Now, I'll try you again. Suppose you were going to carpet a room. Would you use a carpet having a representation of flowers upon it?' ...

'Girl number twenty', said the gentleman, smiling in the calm strength of knowledge.

Sissy blushed, and stood up ...

'If you please, sir, I am very fond of flowers.'

As Charles Dickens concluded: 'Fact, fact, fact, everywhere in the material aspect of the town; fact, fact, fact, everywhere in the immaterial. The M'Choakumchild school was all fact and the school of design was all fact ... world without end, Amen'.

That Charles Dickens had Henry Cole in mind, when he wrote his caricature of the third gentleman, is shown by the manuscript notes he took – about the plot, the characters and the arrangement of the story – now in the Forster Collection at the V&A. Dickens wrote on those notes:

Chapter 1	'Teach these children nothing but facts'
Chapter 2	Mr Gradgrind. Marlborough House Doctrine. Cole. Sissy. Bitzer.

There is even some evidence from the manuscript and proof of *Hard Times* that Charles Dickens toned down his original description of 'the third gentleman', to make it less immediately recognisable as Henry Cole.

'Fact, fact, fact!' said the gentleman with three brisk little claps of his hands. And 'Fact, fact, fact!' repeated Thomas Gradgrind with three confirmatory frowns.'

In the manuscript version, the gentleman was introduced as 'a bustling pleasant little gentleman', 'a glutton', 'an ugly customer' and a man who 'was sure to make opponents where none were ready; by wire-drawing the simplest principle into a complicated absurdity'. In the classroom, he 'complacently smiled' at the children, and spoke 'cheerfully' with 'a blithe sententiousness peculiar to him'. His peroration on birds and butterflies and crockery was considerably longer. And when talking to girl number twenty the gentleman makes a characteristic gesture: 'Fact, fact, fact!' said the gentleman with three brisk little claps of his hands. And 'Fact, fact, fact!' repeated Thomas Gradgrind with three confirmatory frowns.' On the proofs, though, the 'third gentleman' became less genial, less roly-poly, and much more severe; more an embodiment of principles than a flesh-and-blood human being. Maybe the 'bustling, pleasant little gentleman', the 'blithe sententiousness', the over-complication of principles and the 'three brisk little claps ' were a bit too close to the real thing. Because the bustling, pleasant little gentleman was none other than sunny Felix Summerly (a pseudonym of Henry Cole's, as we shall discover later) from the life.

Evidently, Henry Cole later wrote to Dickens – in a surprisingly generous spirit – about this un-named government official in *Hard Times*, the third gentleman, because on 17 June 1854, a couple of months after first publication Dickens tactfully responded:

Dear Mr Cole

... I have in fact retreated to Boulogne to pass the summer in the society of your friend Mr Gradgrind and others, free from the disturbances of London. Otherwise, very readily responding to your good humour, I should have lost no time in calling on Mr Redgrave. [*The artist and teacher Richard Redgrave RA was by then Henry Cole's closest ally, as Art Superintendent.*]

I often say to Mr Gradgrind that there is reason and a good intention in much that he does – in fact, in all that he does – but that he overdoes it. Perhaps by dint of his going his way and my going mine, we shall meet at last at some halfway house where there are flowers on the carpets, and a little standing-room for Queen Mab's chariot among the Steam Engines.

Faithfully Yours,

Charles Dickens

The end of *Hard Times* is very similar. Mr Thomas Gradgrind comes to realise – as he confides, quietly, to his daughter, Louisa: 'I have a misgiving that some change may have been slowly working about me in this house, by more love and gratitude; that what the Head had left undone and could not do, the Heart may have been doing silently.' Or, as the dying and much put-upon Mrs Gradgrind struggles to put into words, on her deathbed: 'Something – not an ology at all – that your father has missed or forgotten, Louisa.' The carnival girl Sissy Jupe, girl number twenty in the schoolroom, who has grown up among the good-natured, slightly crazy circus people, has worked her magic in the Gradgrind household at Stone Lodge, Coketown. Gradgrind's conversion echoes Dickens's words to Henry Cole:

'His character was not unkind, all things considered; it might have been a very kind one indeed, if he had only made some round mistake in the arithmetic that balanced it, years ago'.

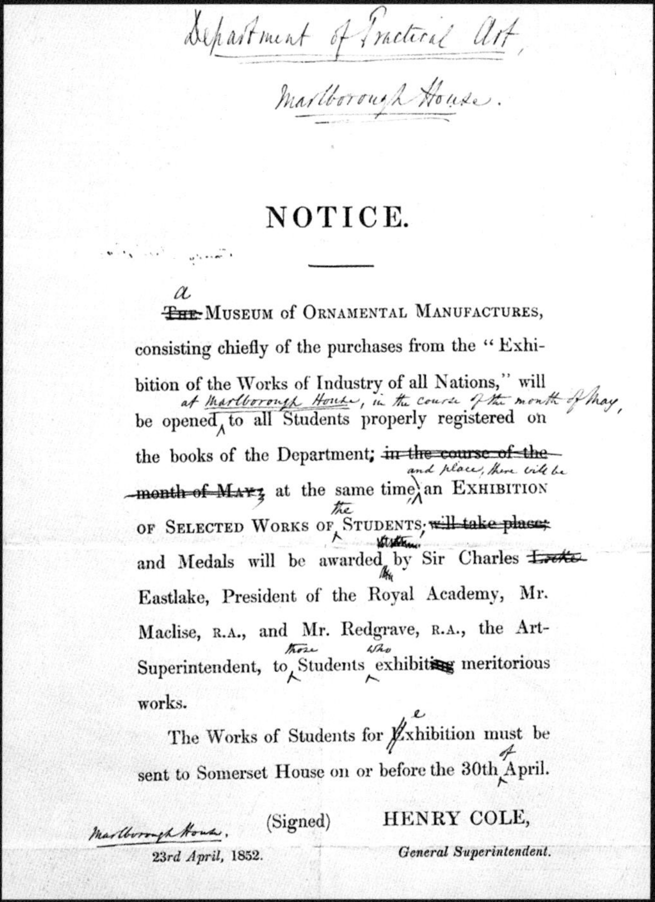

Department of Practical Art,

Marlborough House.

NOTICE.

THE MUSEUM of ORNAMENTAL MANUFACTURES, consisting chiefly of the purchases from the "Exhibition of the Works of Industry of all Nations," will be opened to all Students properly registered on the books of the Department; in the course of the month of MAY; at the same time an EXHIBITION OF SELECTED WORKS OF STUDENTS will take place; and Medals will be awarded by Sir Charles Locke Eastlake, President of the Royal Academy, Mr. Maclise, R.A., and Mr. Redgrave, R.A., the Art-Superintendent, to Students exhibiting meritorious works.

The Works of Students for Exhibition must be sent to Somerset House on or before the 30th April.

Marlborough House,
23*rd April*, 1852.

(Signed) HENRY COLE,
General Superintendent.

A CALL FOR ENTRIES

A notice calling for student exhibits in the 'Museum of Ornamental Manufactures', with amendments by Henry Cole, dated 23 April 1852

A Museum of Ornamental Art

In which Henry Cole persuades friends in high places to let him move the School of Design to Marlborough House, and open a new kind of Museum there too.

The exchange is important, because what Dickens and Cole were really writing about was the origin of this Museum, and where its heart really was: the Marlborough House Doctrine. The 'third gentleman' does not appear again in the novel, after the classroom episode.

Dickens was in fact wrong to suggest a connection between Cole's responsibilities and ordinary schools for children; the Department of Practical Art was solely concerned with design colleges. The one and only function of the 'third gentleman' was to caricature Marlborough House and then exit. Cole had managed in 1852 to cut through the red tape and move most of the Government School of Design from Somerset House in the Strand to Marlborough House in Pall Mall – with strong support from Prince Albert – together with the School's large collection of plaster casts of the greatest hits of European sculpture and decorative art and other objects which the students were expected to copy. And on 19 May 1852 – only a month after his Department had moved in – Cole's Museum opened its doors to the public for the first time in a suite of rooms and galleries on the first floor of Marlborough House. Some of the superfluous ornamental casts were consigned to the cellar, and the kitchen became a lecture hall. The Museum's intended reach was ambitious: the specialised students at the School of Design; manufacturers or members of the manufacturing population who it was felt needed to know about design; and members of the public who it was felt needed to learn about the principles of design so they could become rational consumers. In fact, Cole and friends couldn't settle for a while on the *name* of the Museum, which was an ominous beginning. Was it The Museum of Manufactures, its original name, The

Museum of Ornamental Art – which it soon became – or, as the handbill announcing the opening puts it, a bit of both: a Museum of Ornamental Manufacturing. Branding had yet to be invented. Was it predominantly aimed at the design students or at the trade, or at the public, who came in free on Mondays and Tuesdays? Whoever it was predominantly aimed at, Cole was personally very clear about the heart of the project:

'Taste has its principles as well as morals, which people understand and know… I think to act upon the principle of 'every one to his taste', would be as mischievous as 'every one to his morals'; and I think there are certain principles of taste which all eminent artists are agreed upon in all parts of the world.'

As he added in his first report of the Department on a year in the life of the Museum:

'Notwithstanding the indifference to the principles of Ornamental Art which is too prevalent in the present age … There are signs that the existence of laws and principles in Ornamental Art, as in every branch of human science, is beginning to be recognised. Indeed, without a recognition of them, we feel that Schools of Art can make no progress. Collections of Art will, we think, be most instrumental in helping to form a general belief in these principles.'

So this wasn't a matter of aesthetics: for Cole, it was more like a science, a science which went right back to the Greeks. There were certain basic principles which applied to design, and which could be learned. In the era before Marx and Freud, they were not about sociology or psychology – but about *science*. Cole didn't distinguish between genders, generations, income groups: for him, the phrase 'public taste' was enough.

MARLBOROUGH HOUSE

An illustration of Marlborough House published in John Weale's guide book London Exhibited *in 1851, as the home of the Vernon Collection. The Museum of Ornamental Manufactures moved in during the following year*

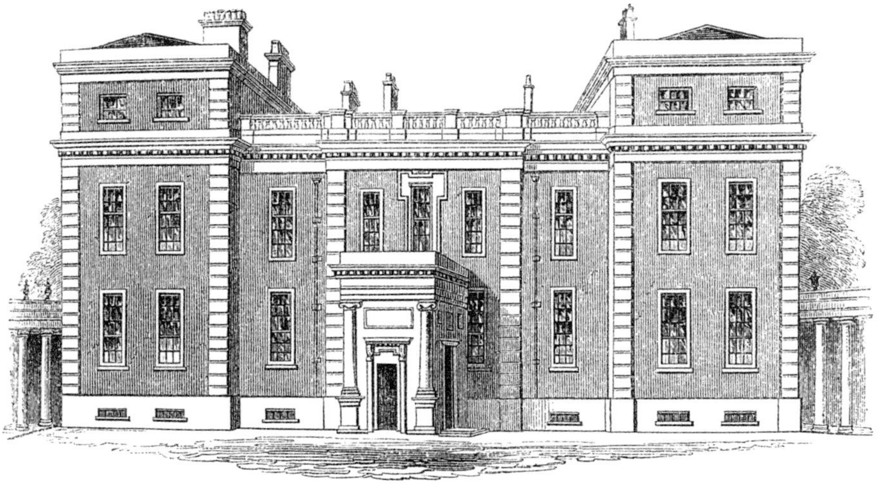

For him, it was indeed fact, fact, fact. The Great Exhibition had shown for all to see that not enough manufacturers or designers in Britain fully understood that science. It had also shown the crying need for a popular 'collection of art' in London. Cole later recalled the state of play in the early nineteenth century:

'The British Museum was jeered at in Parliament as *terra incognita* ... visited by about a hundred visitors a day ... in parties of five persons only ... The state of things outside the British Museum was analogous. Westminster Abbey was closed, except for divine service ... even the Tower of London could not be seen for less than six shillings. The private picture galleries were most difficult of access ... No National Gallery existed ... Kew Gardens were shabby and neglected, and possessed no Museum. Hampton Court Palace was shown, by a fee to the housekeeper, one day in the week.'

Where, he asked, could a youthful artist or designer see examples of the best? Where could manufacturers get their visual education? Where could the public have its taste improved? 'But an immense change has taken place within a recent time ... and the public give manifestations of their wishes throughout the country, which are apparently in advance of the temper of parliament'. A very Henry Cole tactic, that one.In Henry Cole's introductory lecture at the Museum, delivered later in 1852, he talked about the public distinguishing between 'what is good and bad in art'. Design education could help with the supply side, through the Government School and in time its branches; but the demand side – 'the will of the consumer' – was just as important, if not more so. It was not enough to educate the designers. The consumers had to be educated as well. Cole was taking the debates of the *Journal of Design*, the juries of the Great Exhibition, the Government School of Design, and launching them into the public domain, in a very public place.

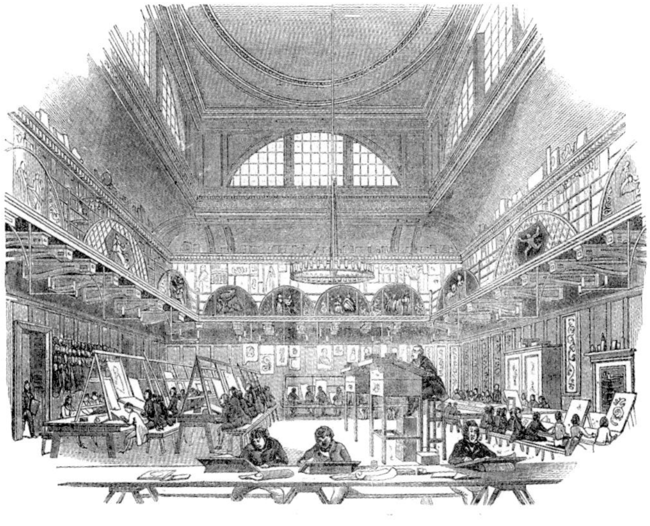

THE GOVERNMENT SCHOOL OF DESIGN

The interior of Somerset House, which housed the Government School, where casts of architectural ornament and antique statuary were collected for the students to copy.

GENERAL PRINCIPLES OF DECORATIVE ART.

The true office of Ornament is the decoration of Utility. Ornament, therefore, ought always to be secondary to Utility.

Ornament should arise out of, and be subservient to Construction.

Ornament requires a specific adaptation to the Material in which it is to be wrought, or to which it is to be applied; from this cause the ornament of one fabric or material is rarely suitable to another without proper re-adaptation.

True Ornament does not consist in the mere imitation of natural objects; but rather in the adaptation of their peculiar beauties of form or colour to decorative purposes controlled by the nature of the material to be decorated, the laws of art, and the necessities of manufacture.

PUBLISHED BY CHAPMAN AND HALL, 193, PICCADILLY, LONDON.

GENERAL PRINCIPLES

One of the Marlborough House placards, explaining the 'General Principles of Decorative Art'

A House full of Horrors

In which visitors to the Museum are exposed, before anything else, to some nightmares of bad design.

Marlborough House opened with a double bill: the annual exhibition of designs by students at the Government School, and some examples of modern manufactured goods – predominantly Indian fabrics and metalwork, French porcelain, Italian cabinet-making, vessels from Turkey and Italy and a few English things as well – purchased with a grant of £5,000, sanctioned by parliament, from the last days of the Great Exhibition of eight months before. £2,000 were spent on 'foreign' products; £1,500 on Indian and less than £1,000 on British. This was the first ever purchase grant the Museum received. The Marlborough House exhibition stayed open for seventeen trial days in May and June 1852 and then closed for the summer vacation and to make 'more permanent arrangements'. This had been, in effect, the inaugural exhibition in the V&A's history. When Marlborough House reopened permanently on 5 September, its holdings in the history of decorative art had been expanded – by exhibits from the Royal Collections and Hampton Court, among others. And it featured a completely new attraction, placed in the corridor leading to the exhibition rooms; this would be the first thing every visitor experienced.

'The ante-room is fitted up as a sort of 'chamber of horrors'

An orientation room. *The Times* on the 6 September reviewed this gallery, which was called 'Decorations on False Principles':

'The ante-room is fitted up as a sort of 'chamber of horrors', with a collection of all kinds of so-called ornamental manufacture, which are considered to exhibit false principles of decoration, such as vulgar and inharmonious colouring, want of meaning and unity in pattern, graceless imitations of natural forms etc. The department, in giving its reasons for condemning the individual examples here shown, afford the public an ample opportunity of testing the accuracy of the canons it enforces in its instruction to students'.

It has been suggested that Cole himself ghosted this article. He was approached by someone later that day, who came up to him and said 'I see your Puff in The Times'. If so, it was he who adapted the phrase 'Chamber of Horrors' from Madame Tussauds to a museum of design. From the wax heads of famous victims of the French Revolution to the education of the eyes of the consumer. He certainly inspired the article. Cole's first report of the Department explained a little more:

'A small portion of the Museum has been fitted up [the same phrase as in The Times] with specimens of all kinds of manufactures, carpets, paper hangings, silks, metals, glass, pottery etc which appear to illustrate departures from those principles of art which are recognised in the department'.

There were 87 items in all.

The exhibits started life as visual aids purchased by the Government School of Design for use in lectures to the students: Owen Jones lecturing on 'true and false principles', Richard Redgrave on 'instruction in Art', John Lindley the botanist on the evolution of design, the evolution of vegetable forms and art botany – not copying what nature presents but what nature does. And they were interspersed with eight large format placards explaining the 'General Principles of Decorative Art', some of them derived from Pugin's two lectures on 'The True Principles of Pointed or Christian Architecture', which had been published some eleven years earlier.[4] These 'True Principles' were sometimes quoted verbatim in the catalogue, under the heading of 'Observations'. Augustus Pugin had in fact joined Cole, Redgrave and Jones

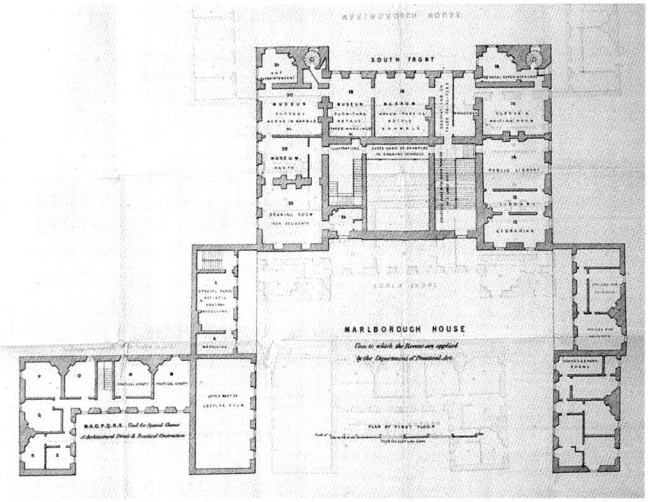

THE CHAMBER

A plan of the main block of Marlborough House in 1852, showing the corridor devoted to 'Decorations on False Principles'. From a lithographic plan printed by Day & Son, included in the First Report of the Department of Practical Art, 1853. Marlborough House also had wings housing rooms that were used by the School of Design.

on the 'Purchases Committee' selecting the objects for the Museum from the 1851 Exhibition – shortly before he fell ill – and they'd argued about quite a number of objects which irritatingly exhibited some good principles and some bad ones, both at the same time. Very irksome.

Skilled workmanship, but defective in the principles of design; crude workmanship, with correct principles of design. Art or workmanship or both. So, should they be purchased for the Museum or not?

In the end, they agreed to differ by saying in the catalogue that 'most examples have a mixed character'.

But the placards had no such doubts: in designed objects, ornament should be appropriate to function (this didn't mean form follows function, but that it was fine to put reeds on a water carafe, if you follow me); ornament should be sympathetic to the material from which the thing is made, and take account of the way it is constructed rather than added on as an afterthought; all beautiful forms relate in some way to the principle of utility; on flat surfaces, ornament should be two-dimensional and not try to be three-dimensional with shadowing; natural forms should be abstracted and formalised rather than directly imitated and shown in perspective – they should be stylised and flat; it was good to use nature as a guide but *never* to try to 'vie with nature'; the forms of the past are never to be copied but only to be studied to understand their formal principles; where possible, geometry and symmetry should be borne in mind, for they are the bases of all ornament. As the third gentleman in Coketown says, with only a little exaggeration, 'you don't walk upon flowers in fact; you cannot be allowed to walk upon flowers in carpets'. And none of this had anything to do with *styles*, they said: it was about 'exemplifying some right principles of construction or of ornament, or some feature of workmanship to which it appeared desirable that the attention of our students and manufacturers should be directed'.

The vocabulary used, in the gallery and in the catalogue – like Pugin's – sometimes had a religious flavour: canons, dogmas, catechisms, doctrines, general belief, missionaries spreading the word to the new branch schools, and leading the errant designer to the path of righteousness. So although this was thought to be a type of human science, it still needed its ten commandments, its creed, and its propagation of the faith. The affordable catalogue – like Felix Summerly's earlier cheap and well-produced museum guides and drawing books – was like an evangelical tract. Cole wrote delightedly that:

'This room appears to excite far greater interest than many objects the high excellence of which is not generally appreciated. Everyone is led at once to investigate the ornamental principle upon which his own carpet and furniture may be decorated, and the greatest benefit to manufacturers may be looked for from the investigation'.

To rub the point in, Owen Jones added:

'There are here no carpets worked with flowers whereon the feet would fear to tread ... no superfluous and useless ornament which a caprice [or fashion] has added and which an accident might remove'.

Perish the thought. Dickens and Jones were clearly reading from the same hymn-sheet.

'Everyone is led at once to investigate the ornamental principle upon which his own carpet and furniture may be decorated...'

One visitor to the exhibition must indeed have been Charles Dickens, and he certainly read and digested the catalogue notes as well. On 4 December 1852 – three months after the reopening – he featured on the front page of his weekly *Household Words*, a magazine for the middle-class domestic reading public, a very amusing article by Henry Morley called 'A House Full of Horrors'. This was about one Mr Crumpet of Clump Lodge Brixton , a quiet City banker whose visit to Marlborough House, and study of the catalogue on the omnibus home convinces him of how incorrect his own taste has been. Mr Crumpet could almost be the prototype for the 'man on the Clapham omnibus' and maybe he was. 'For the last five weeks I have been haunted by the most horrid shapes', he says. 'When I come home a dozen hideous forms glare at me in the hall. My snug parlour maddens me; the walls and floor are densely covered with the most frightful objects; a detestable thing lies spread out at full length before my fire; the persons of my wife and daughter are surrounded very often by these horrors ...

The matter is this: I have acquired some Correct Principles of Taste. Five weeks ago, I went to ... Marlborough House, to look over the museum of ornamental art ...

I had heard of a Chamber of Horrors there established and I found it and went through it with my catalogue. [It was a gloomy chamber, hung round

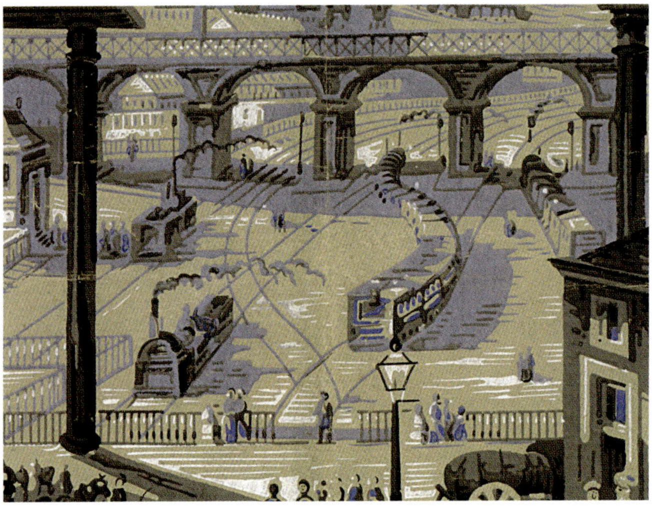

MR CRUMPET'S NIGHTMARE

A detail of the 'wallpaper with a railway station motif...', Exhibit 27 in the 'Chamber of Horrors'

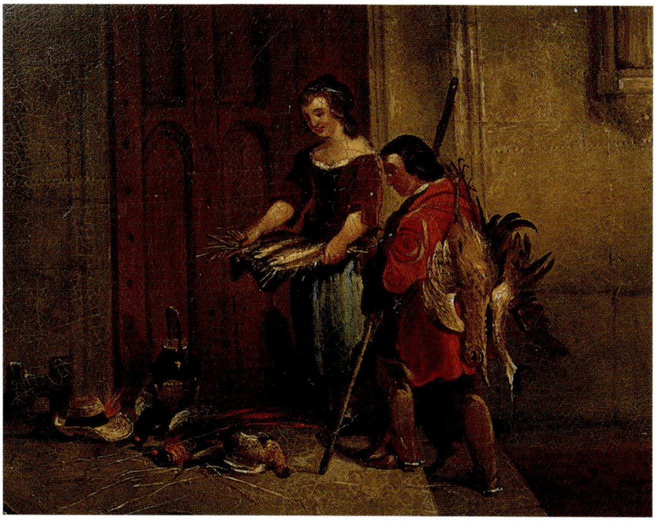

MR CRUMPET'S NIGHTMARE

A detail of the inspiration for the 'tray featuring a bit of one of Landseer's pictures on it ...' Exhibit 79 in the 'Chamber of Horrors'

with frightful objects ... and in each case the catalogue told me why such and such a thing wasn't endurable and I found in the same place also, on equally good authority, in black and white, a few hints of what the correct principles of ornament are ...] I could have cried, sir.

I was ashamed of the pattern of my own trowsers, for I saw a piece of them hung up there as a horror ... The paper in my parlour, sir, contains four kinds of bird of paradise besides bridges and pagodas'.

Mr Crumpet goes to visit his old friend Mr Martin Frippy, a gentleman, at Chimborazo Villa Stockwell, and can't stop himself from commenting on the horrors he encounters there, including several featured in the exhibition: loud check trousers, a handkerchief with Sydenham New Palace on it; wallpaper with a railway station motif, several floral chintzes, on the carpet pictures of thorns and of an ornamental gothic ceiling; a piece of calico with race-horses printed on it; convolvulus blossom on a curtain pole; a tray featuring a bit of one of Landseer's pictures on it and a glass jug with handle in the shape of a cobra. Just as Mr Crumpet is about to distract himself with a consoling cup of tea, he notices with a cry of agony that there's a butterfly painted inside the cup. How horrible! At that point, he has to be taken back to Brixton, a gibbering wreck. Mr Frippy has a more balanced view – like Mr Gradgrind after his conversion and Mr Cole in Dickens's letter:

'I see sense in a good deal of what you have said, though I think it's just a leetle over done ... You have picked up some wholesome views, but you have swallowed them too eagerly and choked yourself ... we say in this country that there's no accounting for taste ...'

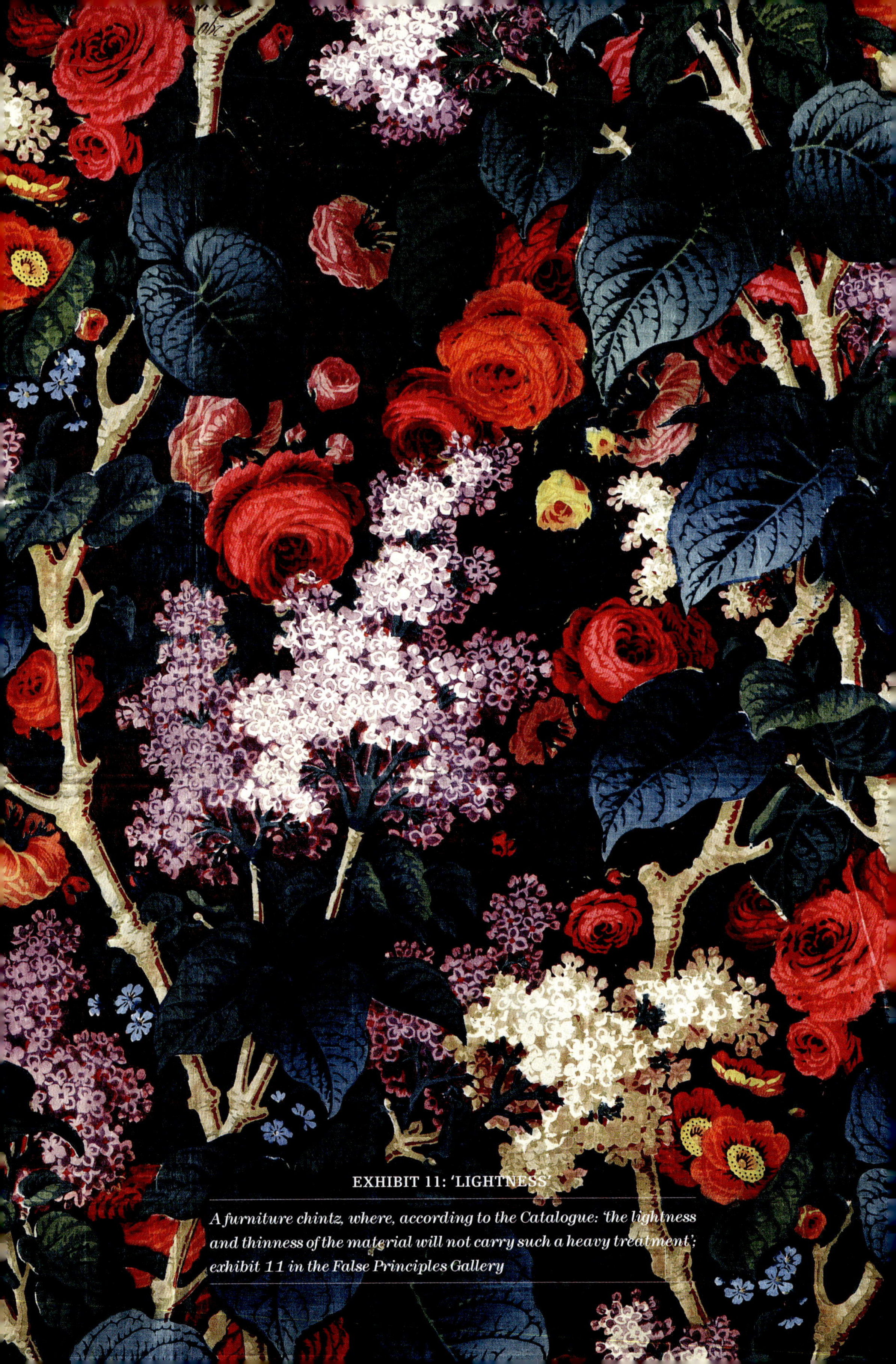

EXHIBIT 11: 'LIGHTNESS'

A furniture chintz, where, according to the Catalogue: 'the lightness and thinness of the material will not carry such a heavy treatment'; exhibit 11 in the False Principles Gallery

Indefensible in principle

In which we are taken, catalogue in hand, on a guided tour of the Chamber of Horrors, with full explanations provided.

The False Principles Gallery has often been mentioned in books, articles and catalogues, but there has never, so far as I know, been a close look at exactly what it contained. One of the problems is that none of the objects seems to have been given a museum number when they were moved from Marlborough House to South Kensington in 1857. It was as if they didn't deserve to be in the collection proper. Some have survived though, or been rediscovered, to become registered since the 1920s – and one or two are even on show in the British Galleries today. The convolvulus gas lamp of 1848 was only identified, in the Museum's stores, as recently as the 1970s – and given a Museum number in 1974, all of 122 years after it was first exhibited as a horror in Marlborough House. The ornate silver candlestick in the style of Louis XV was registered in the year 2000. With a lot of help from curators at the Museum, I've managed to piece together specially for this lecture 17 objects out of the 87 originally shown, or just under a fifth of the exhibition. So, like Mr Crumpet and indeed like Charles Dickens – let us enter Marlborough House, catalogue in hand, and go straight to the gallery marked Decoration on False Principles.[5]

Woven Fabrics & c

We start with one of the display boards, then walk into the first section. 'Woven Fabrics, & c'. Exhibits 1–9 are carpets, including several with flowers directly imitated from nature – and out of scale with each other – one with 'stripes running horizontally, contradicting the lines of the folds in the use of such fabrics' and one featuring pierced Gothic oak panelling and a representation of a moulded surface on it. This was the carpet mentioned in *Household Words*. Then exhibits 10–14 are furniture chintzes: '*Observations.* – Direct imitation of nature; branches of lilac and rose trees made to bend to the forms of sofa cushions and chair arms.'

In other words, these are examples of the cardinal sins of trying to compete with nature, naturalistic floral designs printed on cotton, wrong shading and too much perspective. 'The decoration [of chintzes] seems at present to be of the most extravagant kind', wrote Richard Redgrave in homily mode in the catalogue. '… the lightness and thinness of the material will not carry such a heavy treatment … the use of imitative floral ornament is peculiarly unsuitable on account of the folds, the taste is to cover the surface almost entirely with large and coarse flowers … Nothing can be more erroneous or more essentially vulgar, as would at once be evident did not fashion blind us for a time, and a feeling for costly labour and difficult execution prevail over truth and good taste'. So, false principles. No.12 had been put in the Great Exhibition by one of the most popular furnishing shops in mid-Victorian London, as had No.11. No matter: '… the ground, which should be light in chintzes is entirely obscured by the pattern. General want of repose.' Too dark, too dense, too realistic. Furniture chintzes, numbers 14-16, contain 'wreaths and festoons of natural flowers, tied together with imitations of ribbon,' and 'imitation of one fabric upon another – ribbon upon chintz; the design of the ribbon composed of direct imitations of natural flowers'. No. 16 in addition has 'want of symmetrical arrangement'. Again, false. Then exhibits 17–20 are silk hangings. Such hangings should, said the catalogue, provide a background to the furniture and occupants – completing a domestic picture. The design should be subdued, with not too much contrast, it should be flat and conventionalised. There was a quote from the sainted Pugin's *Christian Architecture* to reinforce this message: 'a moment's reflection must show the extreme absurdity of repeating a perspective over a large surface with some hundred different points of light.'

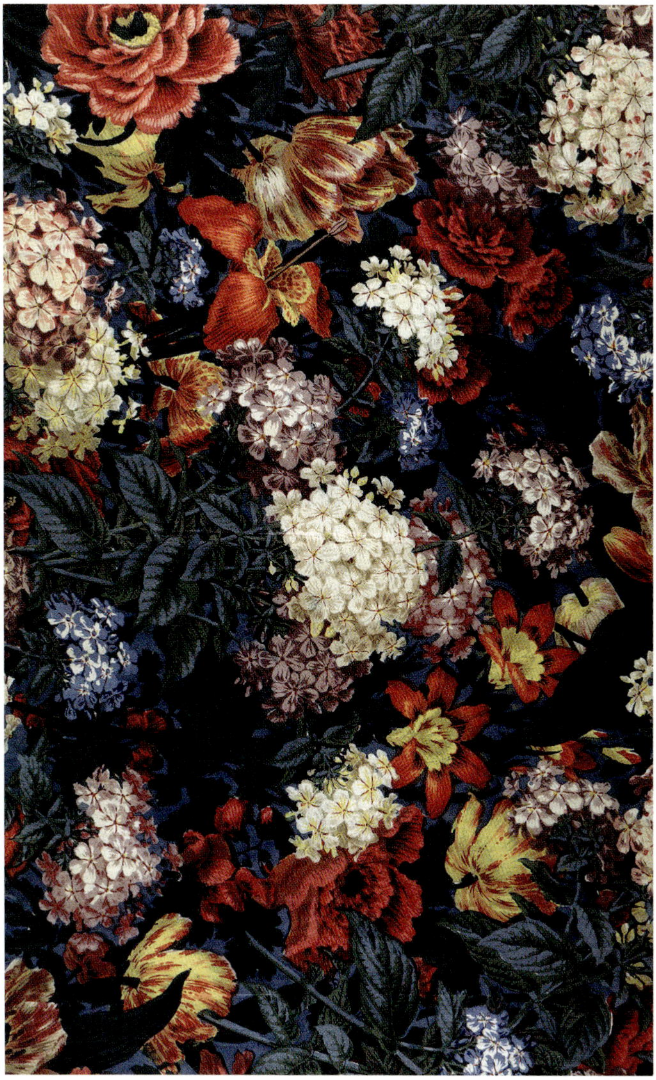

EXHIBIT 12: 'WANT OF REPOSE'

This chintz, showing 'general want of repose', had been shown in the Great Exhibition by a popular furnishing shop; exhibit 12 in the False Principles Gallery

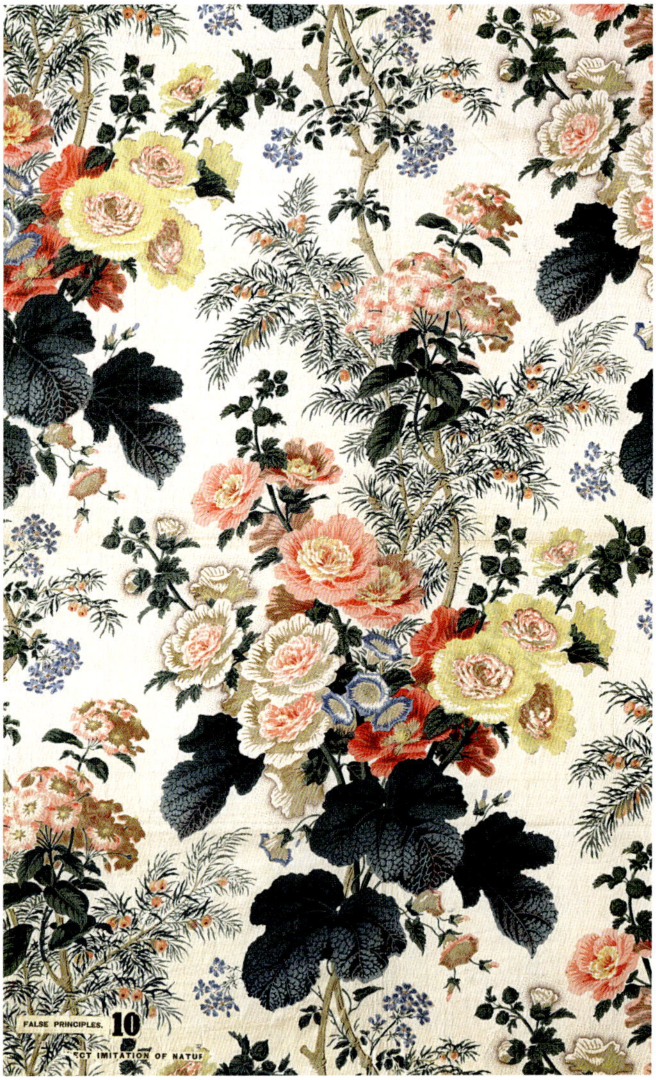

EXHIBIT 10: 'IMITATION'

Furniture chintz guilty of 'direct imitation of nature'; exhibit 10 in the False Principles Gallery.

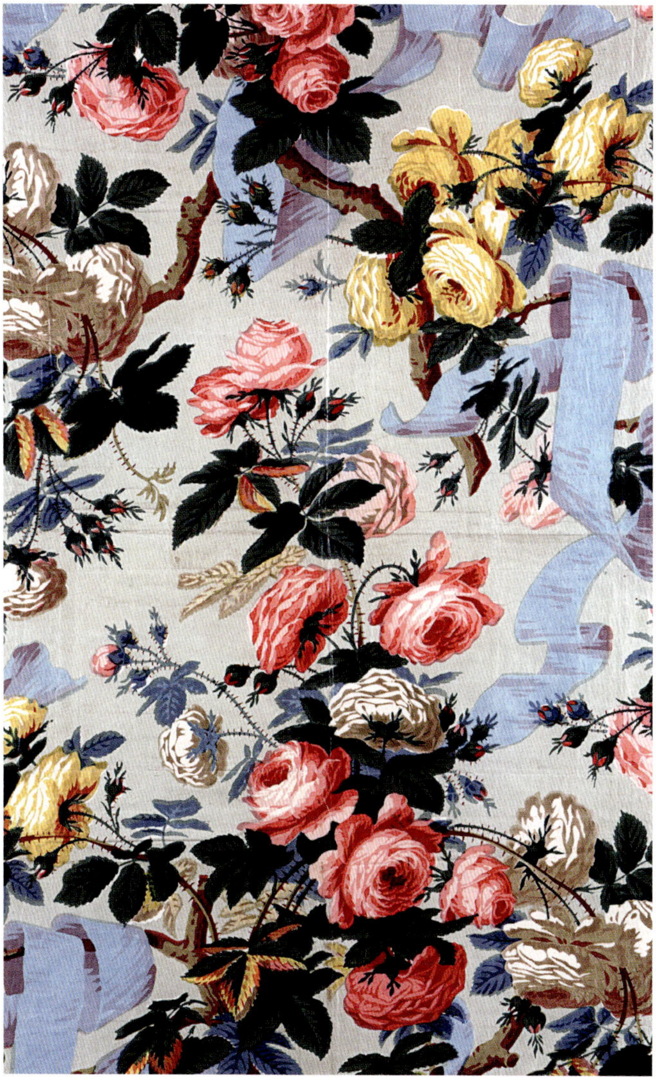

EXHIBIT 16: 'FESTOONS'

This chintz, exhibit 16 in the False Principles Gallery, crammed ribbons and branches and 'festoons of natural flowers' into its design, which overall showed 'a want of symmetrical arrangement'

Paper and Other Hangings

In the second section 'Paper and Other Hangings' are numbers 21 to 36. Most of these were said to be guilty yet again of 'direct imitation of nature', 'natural objects in unseemly positions', or 'imitation of ribbon on paper'. No. 27, for example, showed perspective representations of a railway station, colour printed from wood blocks – a design frequently repeated and falsifying the perspective. *The Builder* magazine took issue with this kind of criticism: it had nothing against pictorial wallpapers as such, it said, so long as they were confined to 'the houses of the humbler classes of society' – and provided their subject-matter was educational.

Unfortunately the railway station wasn't deemed sufficiently educational. Perhaps no 28 was: perspective representation of the Crystal Palace and Serpentine; with flights of steps and architectural framework. No, it was 'causing the same error as No. 27', the railway station. So Great Exhibition souvenir wallpaper was out, as well. As were the two illustrated showing details of Gothic architecture piled on top of one another: No. 31, 'false principle – perspective representation of architecture', and No. 36, also an imitation of Gothic architecture, in this case a busy design of an arch plus figures in red firing rifles and a blue ornate surround.

'*Observations* – objects in high relief; perspective representations of architecture employed as decoration for a flat surface'.

It is interesting that Pugin had published and fiercely attacked another pattern of modern Gothic paper in his *True Principles of Pointed or Christian Architecture*, a wallpaper which has a strong family resemblance to both numbers 31 and 36. And then there is paper hanging number 35 – horses, water and ground floating in the air; landscapes in perspective with race-horses. When the third gentleman in *Hard Times* asks the Coketown schoolchildren 'would you paper a room with representations of horses?', he must have had this very wallpaper in mind. 'Do you ever see horses walking up and down the sides of rooms in reality – in fact? Do you?' Well, here they are – matched up at last. And number 36a has perspective representations of architecture employed as decoration, and, in a different perspective, a battle complete with cavalry charge.

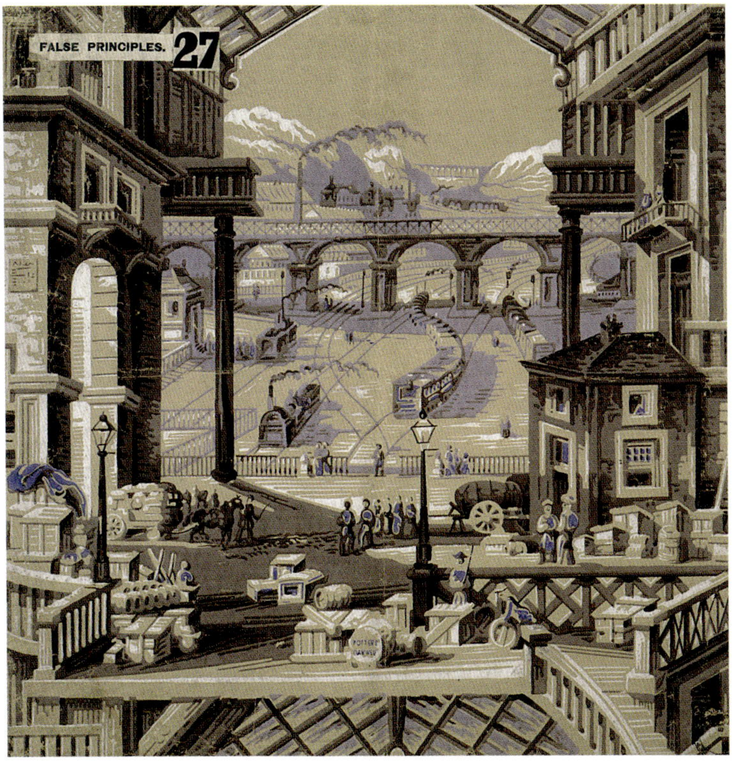

EXHIBIT 27: THE RAILWAY STATION

A wallpaper showing perspective representations of a railway station; exhibit 27 in the False Principles Gallery

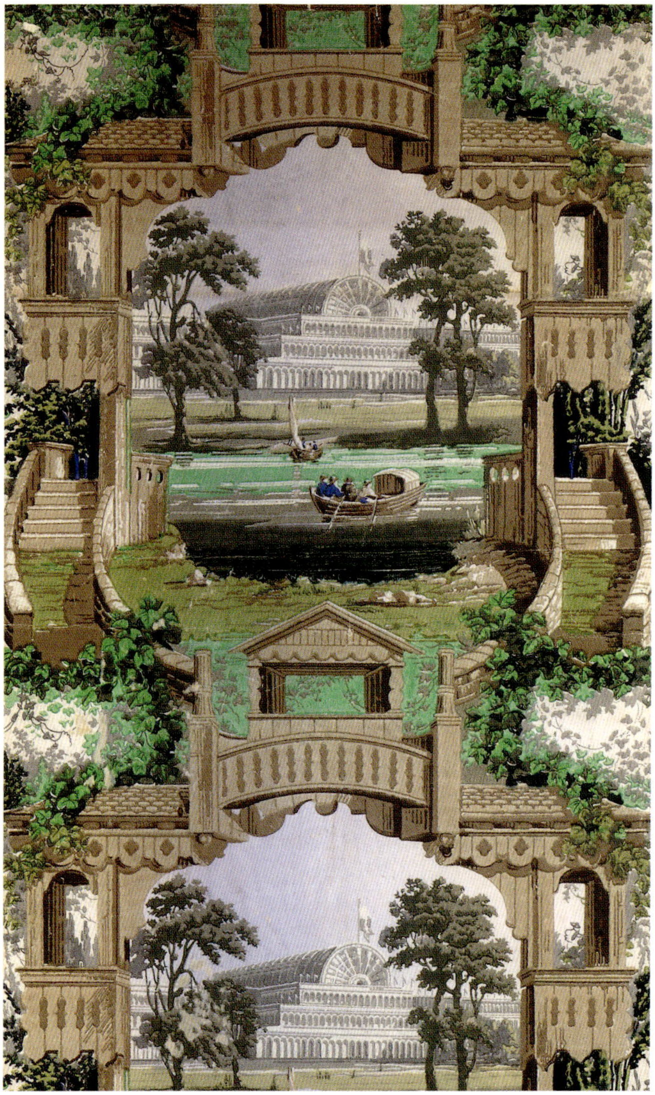

EXHIBIT 28: THE CRYSTAL PALACE

Great Exhibition souvenir wallpaper, showing the Crystal Palace and Serpentine, surrounded by an architectural framework; exhibit 28 in the False Principles Gallery

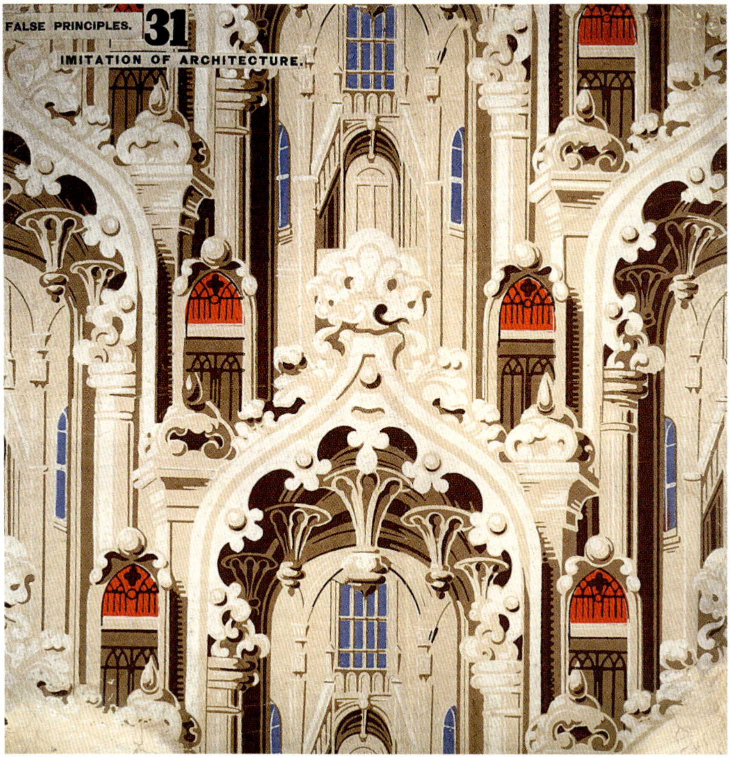

EXHIBIT 31: GOTHIC PILES

Wallpaper with details of gothic architecture piled on top of one another; exhibit 31 in the False Principles Gallery

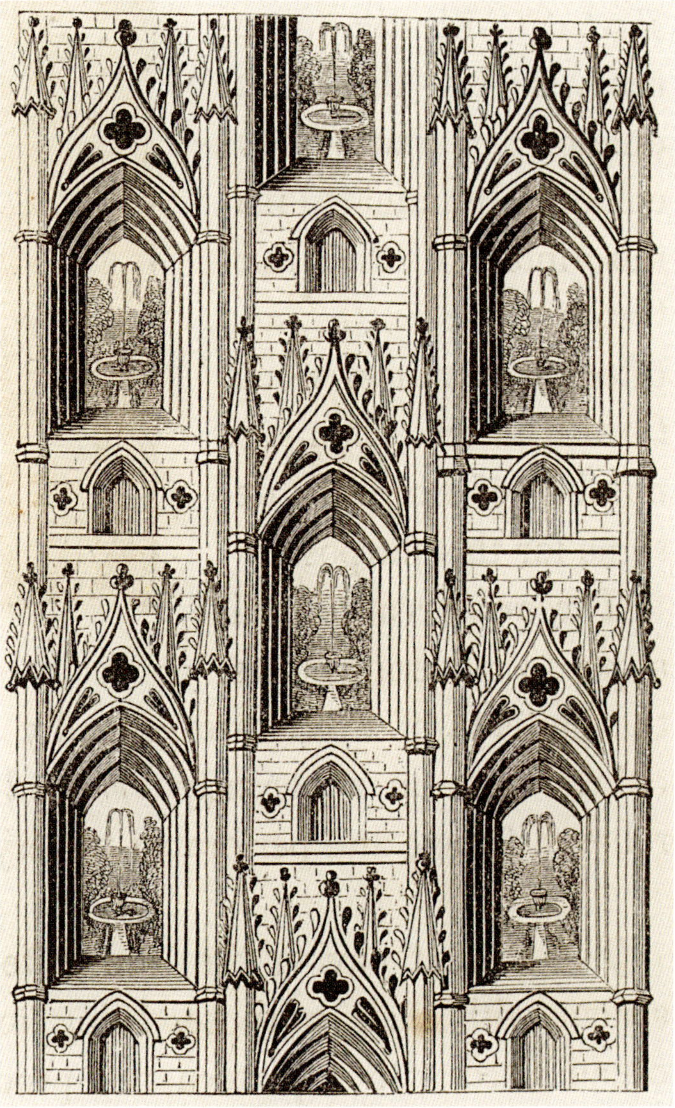

PUGIN'S HORROR

An example of modern gothic wallpaper illustrated and castigated in Pugin's True Principles of Pointed or Christian Architecture

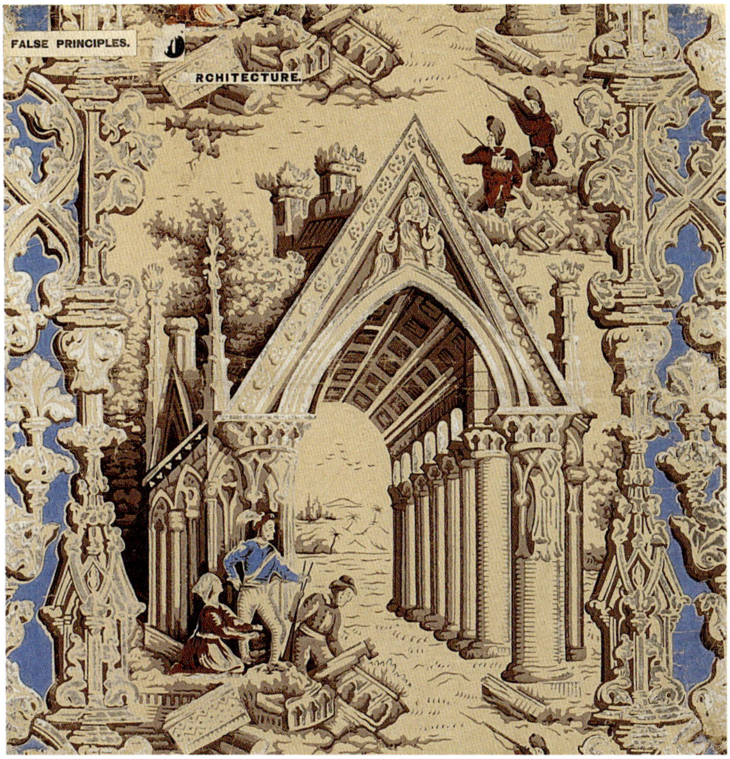

EXHIBIT 36: GOTHIC WITH GUNS

Wallpaper imitating architecture with Gothic arch and figures firing rifles; exhibit 36 in the False Principles Gallery

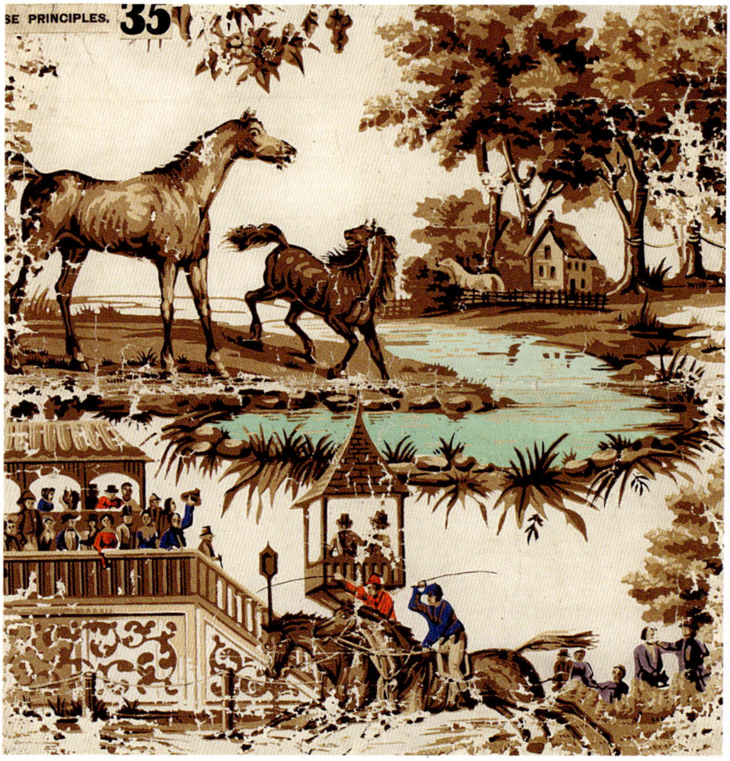

EXHIBIT 35: HORSES

Wallpaper featuring horses, water and landscape floating in the air, with a horse race below; exhibit 35 in the False Principles Gallery: the original of the forbidden wallpaper in chapter two of Hard Times

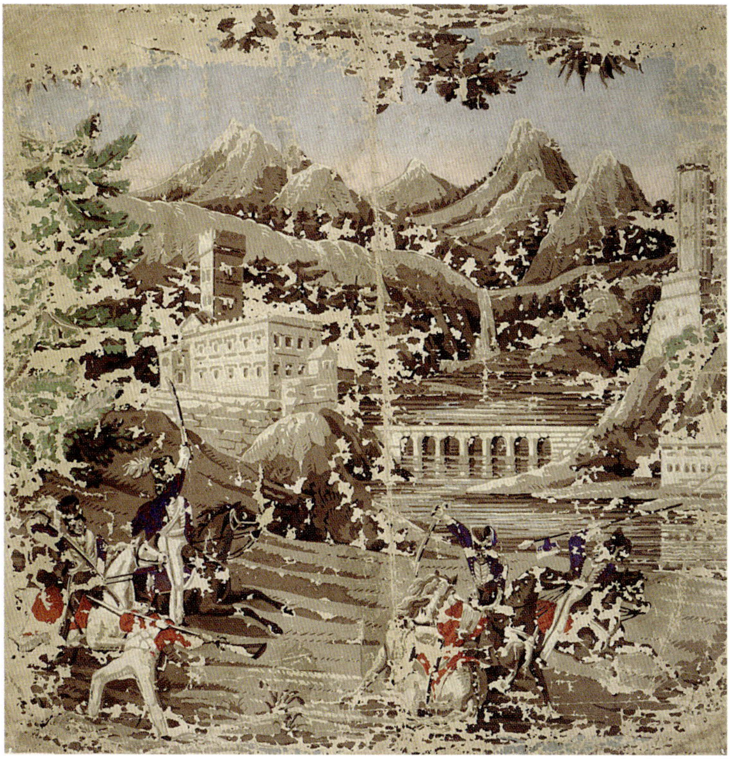

EXHIBIT 36A: CHARGING HORSES

Wallpaper with architecture used as decoration and a cavalry charge for good measure; exhibit 36a in the False Principles Gallery

Garment Fabrics

In the third section 'Garment Fabrics', are numbers 37–60a, with examples of gaudy, florid or over-large designs – over-ornamentation, violent contrasts, and not enough account taken of the material and folds, according to Richard Redgrave's introduction. For example, coarsely striped shirts or trousers, sometimes with outlandish designs on them, like Mr Martin Frippy's. 'No.s 50, 51, 52 – Calico for Shirts. *Observations.* – Direct imitations of figures and animals; ballet girls, polka dancers and race horses. No.s 53, 54, 55, 56 – Patterns for trowsers. *Observations.* – Geometrical forms totally unfit for the garment for which they are intended; interfering with the form of the wearer.' Sadly no items have yet been found surviving from this section.

Porcelain, Glass, Metal Work & c.

Numbers 61–87 are in the 'Porcelain, Glass, Metal Work & c' category. Here are the only illustrations to be found in the 'False Principles' catalogue, one of a Jelly Glass No. 64 – 'the natural outline of the glass when blown completely destroyed by the surfaces being cut' – and one of a Glass Flower Vase No. 69: 'the general outline entirely destroyed by the vertical cuttings'. In general, Redgrave wrote, 'brilliancy of surface, transparency and lightness should ever be preserved' in glass – rather than ground ornament, deep surface-cutting and opaqueness, all of which 'tend to vulgarize'. The other items mentioned in the catalogue include a butter dish, a wine glass, some goblets, vases and at the bottom of the page a pair of scissors imitating a stork, with the body of the bird breaking in half when the scissors are opened. 'Imitation of a stork; the beak opening the reverse way; the body of the bird made to open in the direction of its length.'

At No. 79, we have a papier-mâché tray – an example of popular taste, presenting numerous features which 'students should carefully avoid' because it has just about everything wrong with it. At the centre is 'the piracy of a picture' in the collection of the Duke of Devonshire. The picture, on which much labour has been bestowed by the artist, is 'thrown away' when the tray is in use: it will be covered with what's being served. The scroll lines of the ornament don't follow the outer form – in that they are 'scattered as if by chance anywhere'. And the glitter of the mother of pearl, the most prominent feature, does not go with either the gilt border or with the painting. All in all, this tray is so 'ill arranged that it creates the impression that the article is slopped with water or perforated with holes.' Henry Morley's reference to 'a tray with a bit of one of Landseer's pictures on it' – found in Mr Frippy's Stockwell Villa – is evidently a reference to this papier-mâché tray, which was manufactured in Birmingham.

Finally, exhibit numbers 80 to 87 are in a section mainly devoted to 'Metal Work', a section that begins with another quotation from Pugin's *Christian Architecture* on ornament being applied wrongly to disguise not beautify an article of utility – 'extravagance [used] to conceal the real purpose for which the article has been made.' Redgrave added 'it has often been remarked that the figures introduced into the ornament of metal-work are too often hereby applied or stuck on, not arising out of the work as a constructed whole…' Exemplified by, it seems, No. 80, a brass and white glass curtain rod holder – one of a pair – in the shape of an open flower with leaves. 'Direct imitation of nature; and unfitness for the purpose. Yet this, of its kind, has been one of the most successful articles of manufacture in respect of sale.' Or No. 83, the gilt, brass and glass Gas Burner. 'Gas flaming from the petal of a convolvulus!' shrieks the catalogue. ' – one of a class of ornaments very popular but entirely indefensible in principle'. This was yet another example of the 'ignorant search after the merely novel' and was 'in the worst possible taste for any useful purpose.' It, too, as it happened was manufactured in Birmingham in 1848. Or No. 85, which was an opal liquor bottle in the shape of a pink snake. That one sounds very strange. 'Observation: The transference of glass as a material is disregarded and the snake introduced as an ornament is out of place, and has no connection with form or structure.' Just like Mr Frippy's glass jug with a handle in the shape of a cobra.

No. 86, an earthenware Bread Plate, was made especially for the Great Exhibition by a firm in Stoke-on-Trent to show off the latest developments in polychrome painting and printing. It shows in realistic detail Christ and the Pharisees, with a quotation round the neck from Matthew, Chapter 12 Verse 57. Whatever its scriptural credentials, the catalogue observed:

'A very good example of printing applied to the decoration of pottery, but the surface being wholly covered is objectionable, and the religious picture, besides being out of place in the centre of a bread plate, and the mottos [are] very inappropriate to the intended use'.

Maybe a citation of the Feeding of the Five Thousand would have made things a little better, with ornament more appropriate to function – such as the serving of fish sandwiches. Or maybe not.

So to the final exhibit, No. 87, an electroplated silver candlestick in the style of Louis XV:

'*Observations* – An example of the extreme faults of this style; symmetrical arrangement being rejected as a principle, and structured form disregarded, the whole appears the result of chance rather than design. The base is formless, confused and too heavy for the stem, which in its turn is structurally broken in two places; the socket has no determinate form, and does not correspond to the cup inserted into it; all that is obtained by this sacrifice of structural and ornamental principles, is the mere glitter of metal'.

FALSE PRINCIPLES.

Examples of False Principles in Decoration.

No. 62.—GLASS BUTTER DISH.

No. 63.—WINE GLASS.

No. 64.—JELLY GLASS.

Observation.—In each of these articles the natural outline of the glass when blown destroyed by the surfaces being cut.

No. 65.—GLASS GOBLET, OPAL.

Observation.—Coarse form; the transparency of the material sacrificed to imitate alabaster.

No. 66.—GLASS GOBLET (FLASHED WITH OPAL AND ENGRAVED).

Observations.—Transparency, which constitutes the beauty of the material, entirely destroyed, thereby rendering it impossible to see the contents.

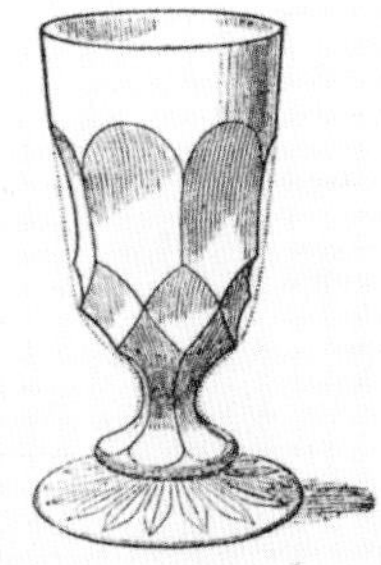

No. 64.

No. 67.—GLASS GOBLET.

Observation.—Form unfitted for use; the vessel shrinks in the middle so that it could not be emptied without raising the foot considerably above the mouth.

No. 68.—CORNUCOPIA FOR FLOWERS.

Observations.—The constructive line very bad,—the base appearing as if stuck on, instead of forming part of the whole; transparency of the material destroyed.

No. 69.—GLASS FLOWER VASE.

Observation.—The general outline entirely destroyed by the vertical cuttings.

No. 70.—EARTHENWARE VASE.

Observation.—Ornaments copied from a funeral vase, and inappropriate (see observations, No. 81).

No. 71.—FLOWER-POT.

Observation.—Imitation in earthenware of reeds, painted blue, bound together with yellow ribbon.

No. 72.—PAIR OF SCISSORS.

Observations.—Imitation of a stork; the beak opening the reverse way; the body of the bird made to open in the direction of its length.

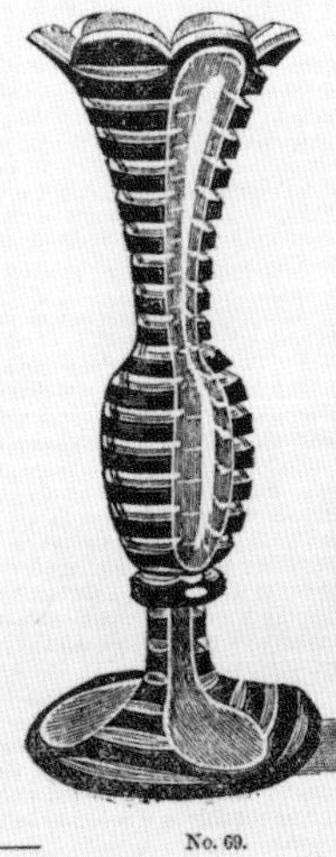

No. 69.

21

EXHIBITS 64 AND 69: THE ORIGINAL CATALOGUE

The only illustrations in the False Principles catalogue, showing a Jelly Glass (exhibit 64) and a Glass Flower Vase (exhibit 69)

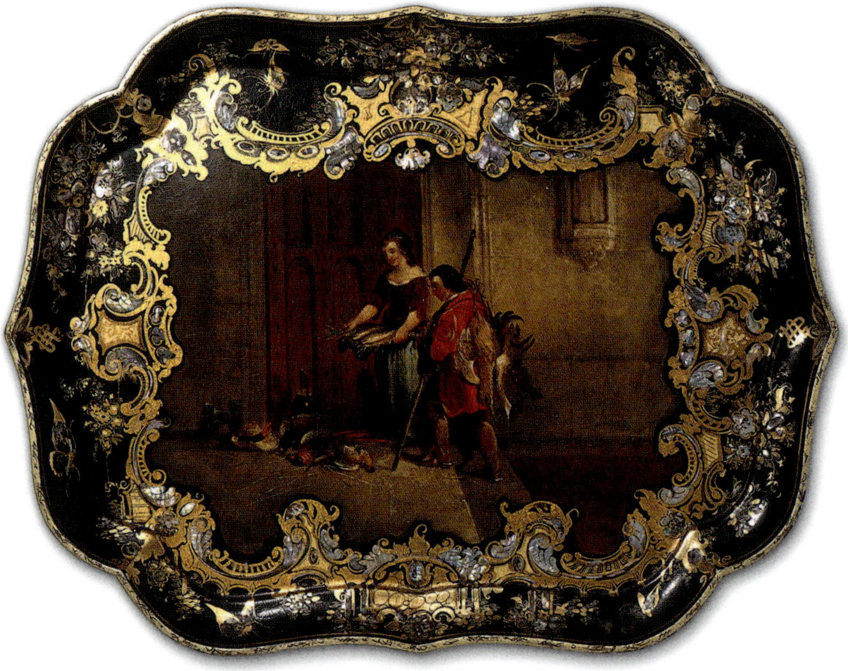

EXHIBIT 79: 'ILL-ARRANGED...'

A papier-mâché tray, with 'the piracy of a picture' in the centre and elaborate gilt border; exhibit 79 in the False Principles Gallery

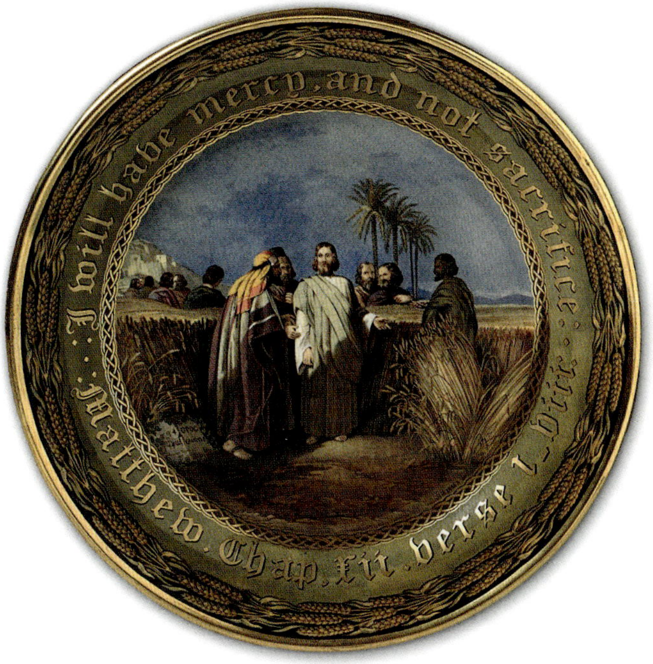

EXHIBIT 86: 'INAPPROPRIATE...'

Earthenware Bread Plate, showing – in virtuoso polychrome – Christ and the Pharisees, made especially for the Great Exhibition. Exhibit 86 in the False Principles Gallery

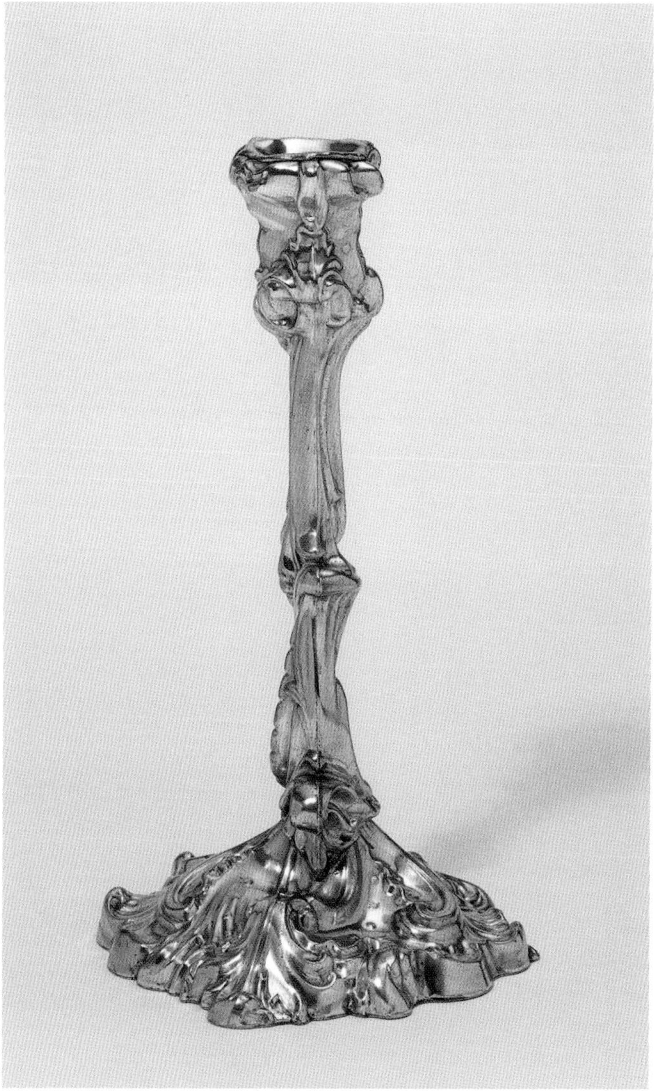

EXHIBIT 87: 'CHANCE RATHER THAN DESIGN...'

Ornate electroplated silver candlestick in the style of Louis XV – 'an example of the extreme faults of this style'. Exhibit 87, the final exhibit, in the False Principles Gallery

Mr Crumpet – his head crammed full of true and false principles – did not make it into the Museum Rooms proper where the displays belonged to a different world. The Chamber of Horrors featured 'objects of daily use', 'articles such as are of daily production which are remarkable for their departure from every law and principle and some even from the plainest common sense in their decoration' – within the reach of those with 'poor to moderate means'. The rest of the Museum by contrast was concerned with exemplary, virtuoso objects from the Great Exhibition, fine pieces from the Royal Collection – presented as if in a connoisseur's cluttered, romantic interior – and selections for the plaster casts which had first been used as teaching aids in the Government School. These different displays matched the different public audiences Marlborough House aimed to reach. But Mr Crumpet would have staggered straight home, exhausted and ashamed of his own trousers – resolved, when he could afford it, as he himself says, to send Mrs Crumpet's best gown to the gentlemen of the Museum as a *particularly* choice example of a horror.

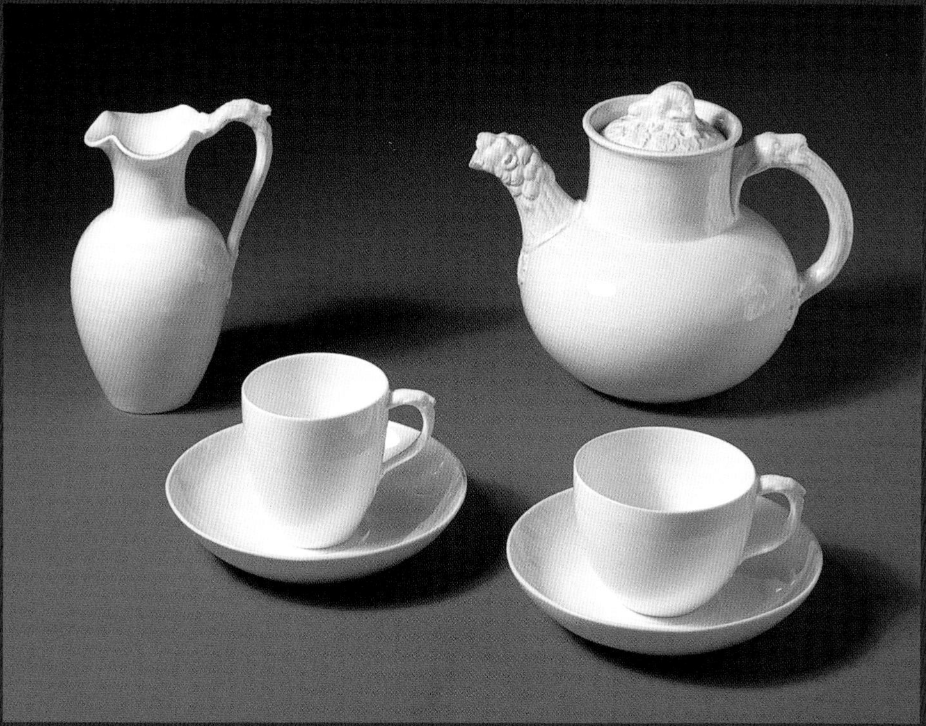

AN ETRUSCAN TEA SET

A tea set in Etruscan style designed by 'Felix Summerly' and shown at the second Society of Arts exhibition of manufactures

The Etruscan Tea Set

In which we learn at last about Henry Cole's own taste in design, and discover that it is not as easy as he thought to tell the difference.

Much has been made in the literature of these true and false principles, especially since Nikolaus Pevsner hailed them in the 1930s as distant prophecies of the Modern Movement in architecture and design. But the closer one looks, the less modern – and even consistent – they become.

It is worth pausing for a moment to compare the Chamber of Horrors with Henry Cole's own taste at this time, insofar as we can recover it. Cole was unique among senior civil servants involved in art education – then or now – in that he had actually taken a course in watercolour under David Cox when young, and his sketches had been exhibited at the Royal Academy. We have seen his etchings of the terrier Jim. His design work was shown, from the mid-1840s onwards, under his favourite pseudonym of Felix Summerly – Felix meaning happy, Summerly meaning sunny: very Henry Cole – and his best-known piece was his inexpensive Etruscan tea-set which won silver at the second Society of Arts exhibition of manufactures. Having decided to enter, to understand the deep principles of tea sets, Cole went straight to the British Museum:

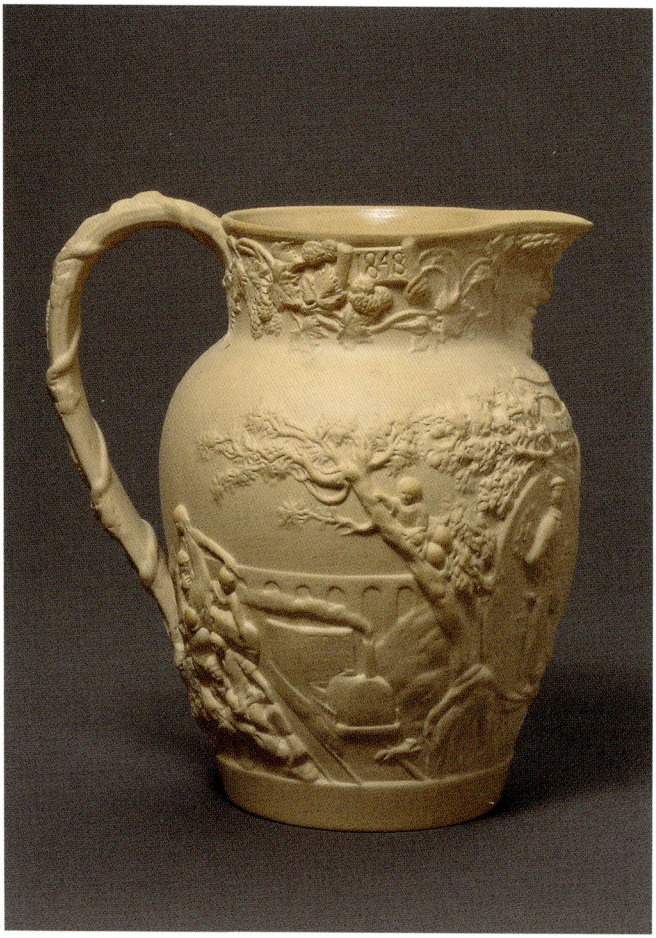

THE TWO DRIVERS

Henry James Townsend's jug 'The Two Drivers - past and present' (1847), designed originally in white stoneware, and later coloured, for Summerly's Art Manufacturers - with a strong emphasis on the 'Art'

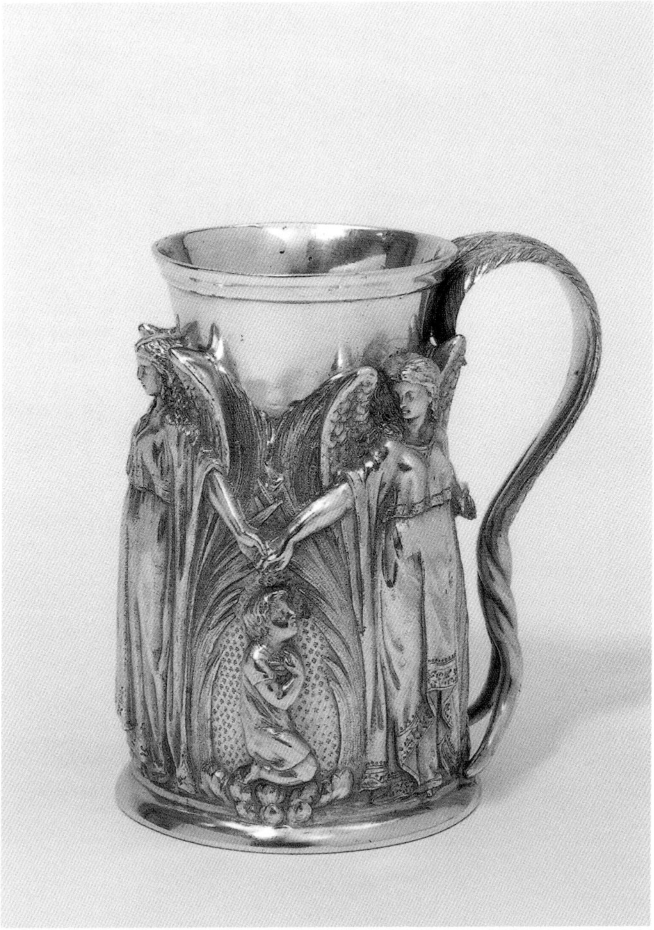

REDGRAVE'S CHRISTENING MUG

A silver christening mug, heavily embossed with guardian angels, originally designed by Richard Redgrave for Felix Summerly's Art Manufactures in 1847, and featured in Cole's first catalogue. This particular example was made much later, in 1865, especially for the museum. Form follows function? The mug is not easy to drink from, though the angels are appropriate to the occasion.

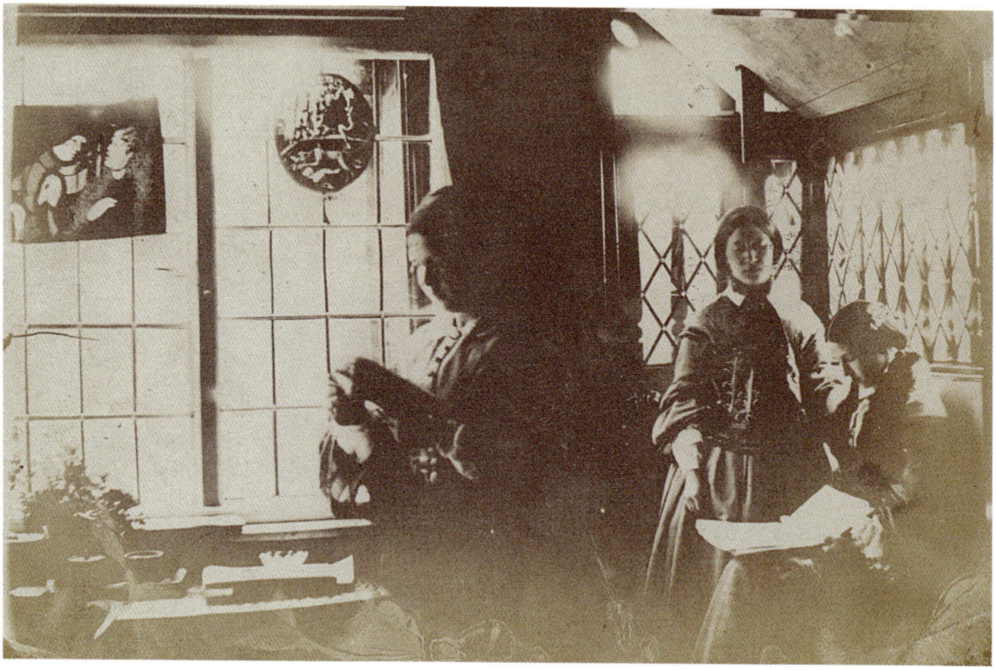

ELM COTTAGE, DRAWING ROOM

A photograph taken by Henry Cole in May 1856 of his three daughters in the cluttered drawing room of Elm Cottage in Shere, Surrey

'The forms in principle are new combinations of the best Etruscan Pottery, with ornaments at the handles etc superadded [*sic*] and designed so as not to interfere with the simplicity of the outlines ... The Milk Pot has three lips like some articles of Etruscan Pottery.'

He then visited Herbert Minton at his Pottery in Stoke-on-Trent, and with a little technical help, manufactured the set in red unglazed clay – which was how it was originally exhibited. Prince Albert ordered one for use on the breakfast table at Balmoral. The whole experience 'strengthened my conviction that an alliance between fine art and manufacturers would promote public taste', and Cole was to present a set to the Museum 'as a link in the circumstances leading to that Great Exhibition, which sowed the seeds for the beginnings of the ... Museum itself.' This certainly isn't an example of proto-Modernism – in retrospect, it too is a characteristic product of its time, with its Greek historical references; its urge to tell a story; its showing off, though admittedly not as much as some of the pieces in the Chamber of Horrors. At the time, Summerly's 'Art Manufactures'

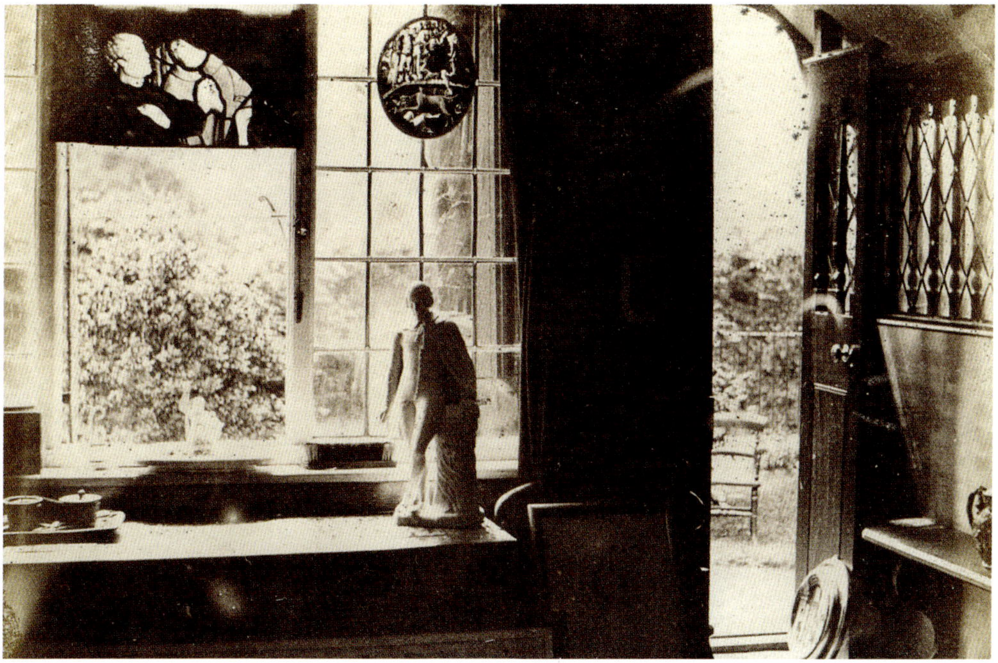

ELM COTTAGE, DRAWING ROOM

The cottage's drawing room, with inset fragments of stained glass and a Parian-ware Shakespeare on the table

were treated as earnest attempts at design reform, well enough known for *Punch* to satirise them in 1847, with a cartoon of various 'humble objects' in the shape of distended human beings – a reference to Cole and friends going at it 'poker and tongs'. In retrospect, the distinctions between Cole and mainstream are more difficult to draw.

Another, more personal example of Henry Cole's own taste in the 1850s is evidenced by the fascinating series of snaps he took on 18 May 1856 of the drawing room and bedroom at Elm Cottage, his country retreat in Shere, Surrey.[6] These photos were made in the year he purchased the very first example of the art of photography for the Museum's collection; and they were acquired by the V&A as recently as 1987 to add to that collection. There are three photos of the drawing-room – some with watercolour retouches – and one of the bedroom. The contrast between daylight and the dark interior is not always successful but the glimpse of Cole's domestic arrangements is fascinating. The interiors are filled with the clutter of pictures and ornaments – plus Cole's carefully posed daughters

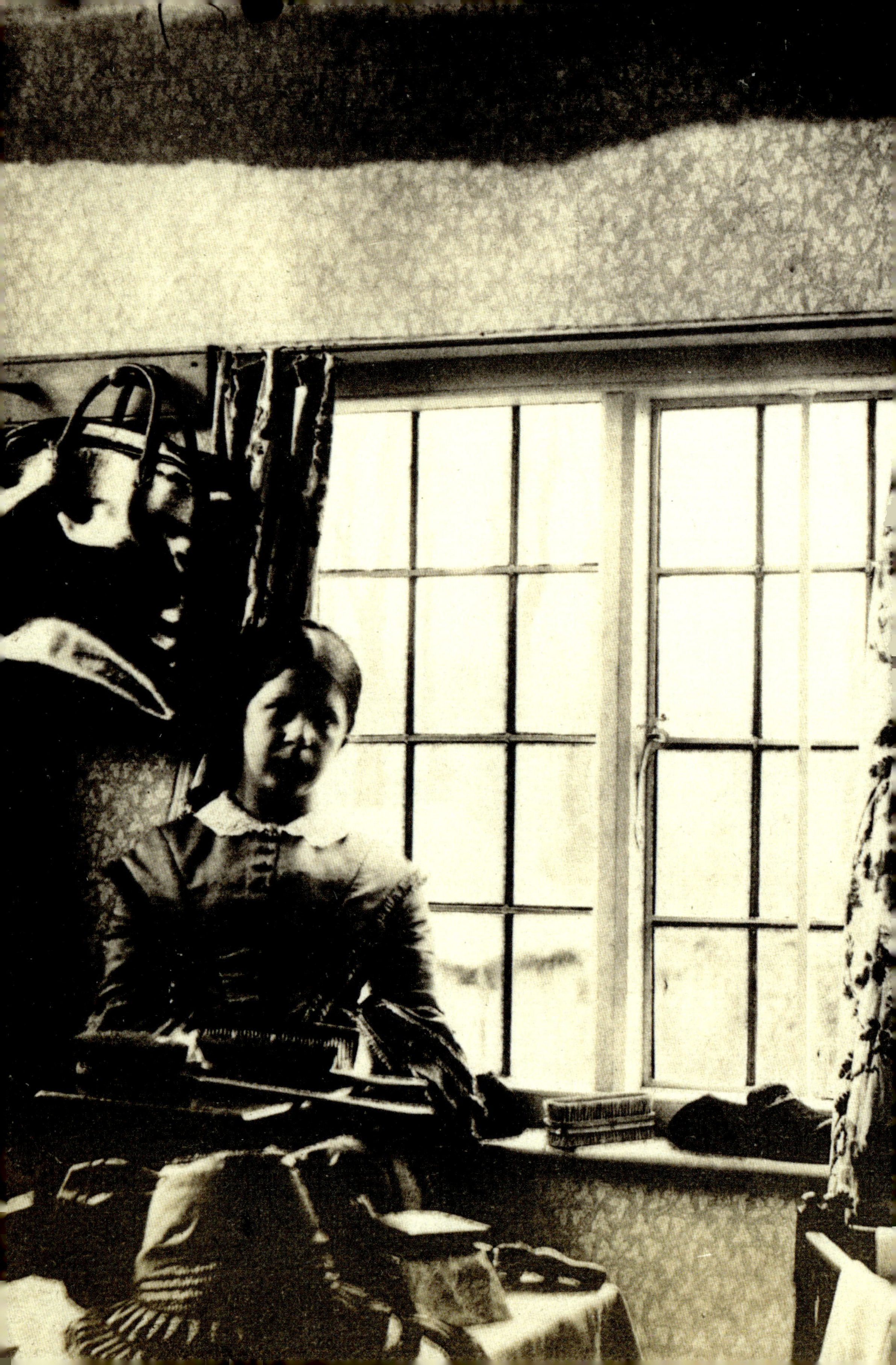

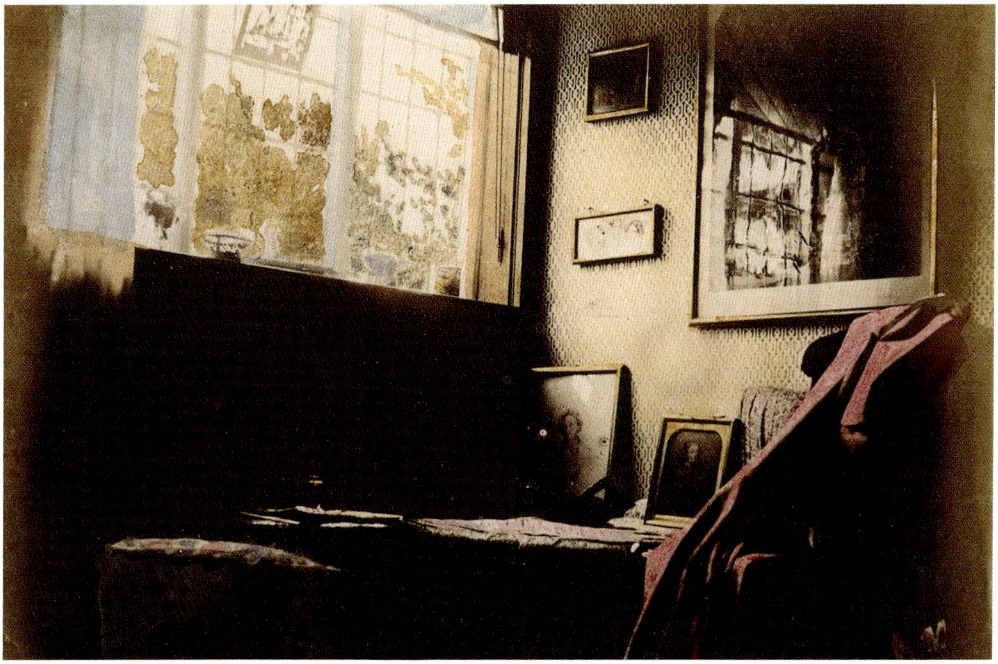

ELM COTTAGE, BEDROOM

Cole's photograph of the cottage's bedroom, with his daughter Mary surrounded by busy curtains and wallpaper

ELM COTTAGE, DRAWING ROOM

A corner of the cottage's drawing room

Mary, Tishie (middle) and Hennie (seated). A surprising, almost bohemian, kind of clutter. One of the drawing-room photographs, has a framed lithograph of the nave of the Crystal Palace on the right, a portrait of Cole in his twenties, and geometrical, flat wallpaper – which he'd selected in London, with Richard Redgrave there for moral support, on 22 February 1856. Another of the drawing-room has inset fragments of stained glass in the window, and on the table a Parian-ware Shakespeare and one of the rarer products of Felix Summerly's Art Manufactures, the 'Bride's Inkstand'. In the only bedroom photograph, Cole's daughter Mary stands, surrounded by busy curtains, the wallpaper once again, and Shaker-style pegs for hanging things up, on the left. Again, not exactly proto-Modernism, although the wallpaper does indeed obey some of the Marlborough House commandments: it doesn't imitate nature, it repeats well, and it takes account of the dimensions of the room. Illustrated are two other examples of good principles, by Cole's advisers: Richard Redgrave and Augustus Pugin. Redgrave's 'wellspring' water carafe 1847-50 created for Felix Summerly's Art Manufactures: reeds on a carafe were, as we have seen, acceptable;

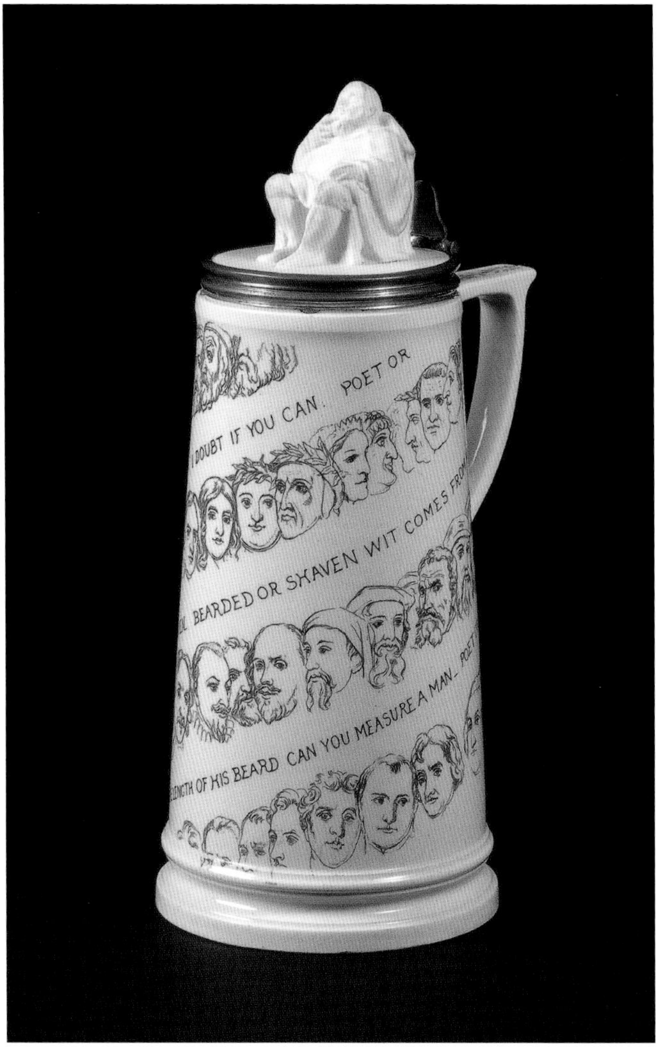

REDGRAVE'S HEROES

Richard Redgrave's 'Heroes Bearded and Beardless' Shaving Mug (1848), is one of the earliest designs for Felix Summerly's Art Manufactures- complete with improving message and narrative subject-matter. This example was made by Wedgwood in 1865

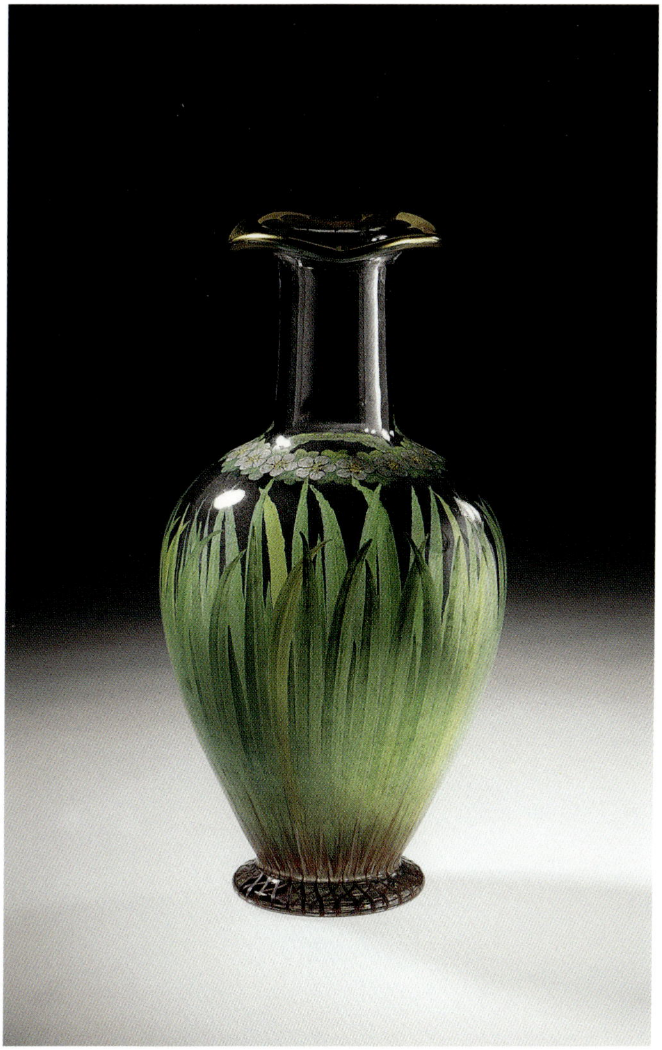

THE WELLSPRING

Richard Redgrave's glass 'wellspring' water carafe, with a design based on reeds, 1847-50

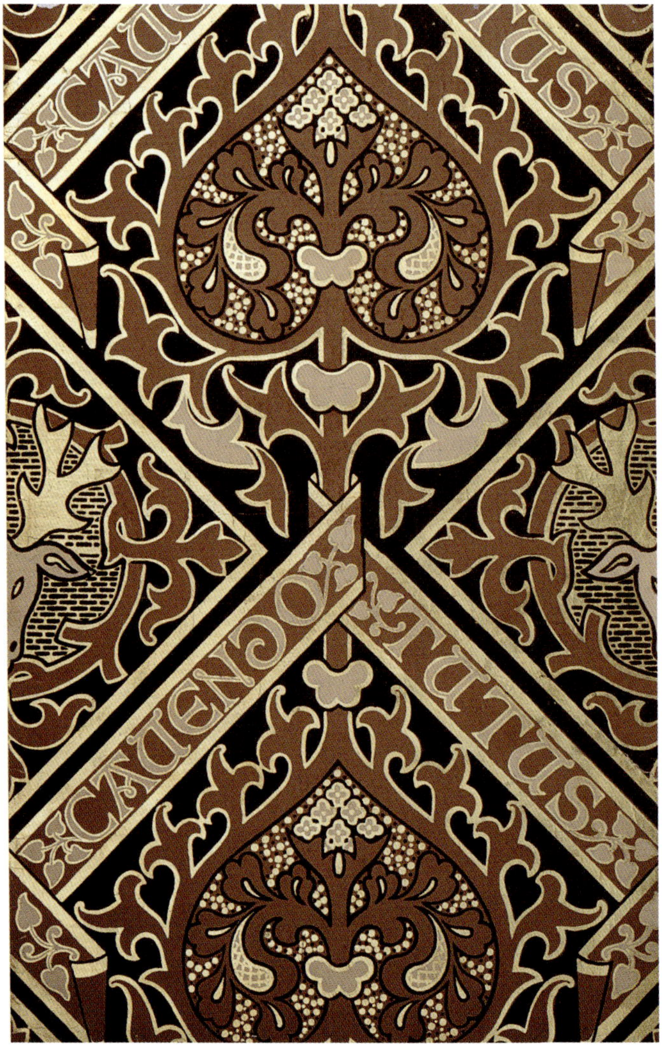

'CORRECT' GOTHIC WALLPAPER

A rich wallpaper design by Pugin, called 'Lismore' and dating from 1851

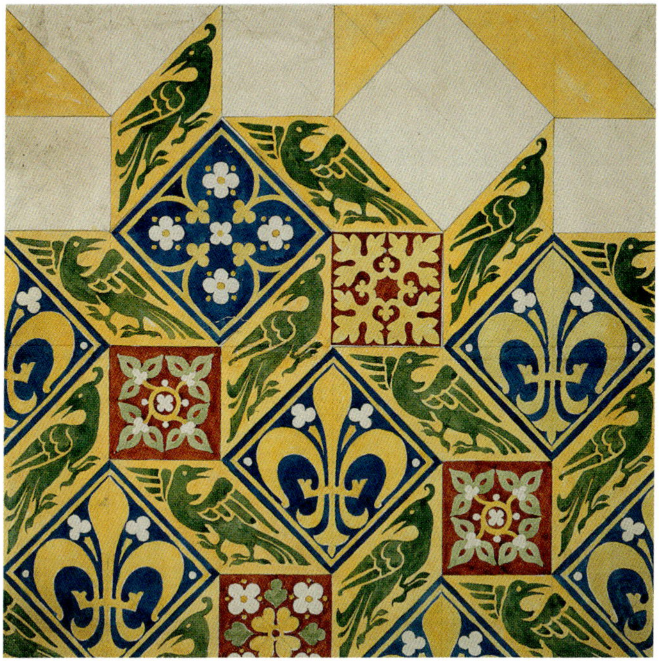

'CORRECT' GOTHIC TILING

A tile design by Pugin for the Houses of Parliament, 1852

a liquor bottle in the shape of a pink snake was not. Ornament appropriate to function was fine. And two Pugin wallpapers: one designed in 1851; the other in 1850 for Duke of Devonshire in Co. Waterford. Also shown are a Pugin wallpaper designed in 1851 and his designs for tiles for Parliament (1852). Again, the distinction is more subtle in retrospect than it evidently appeared at the time.

The Chamber of Horrors finally closed in June 1853, after ten months (not after two weeks, as some of the books and web sites say). Mr Crumpet evidently visited it at the end of October or beginning of November 1852, *Household Words* published the articles in December and the first instalment of *Hard Times* was issued at the beginning of April 1854, ten months after the gallery closed. According to Henry Cole, although the Chamber had proved a big public success – and certainly a talking point around town– the manufacturers had 'raised an outcry'. John Bright MP had written to him saying that the Museum was an out-and-out attack on free trade: 'You are aiming at what is unnecessary and at much that is impossible... [I] don't see where your principle, if good at all, is to stop.' A Manchester economist had

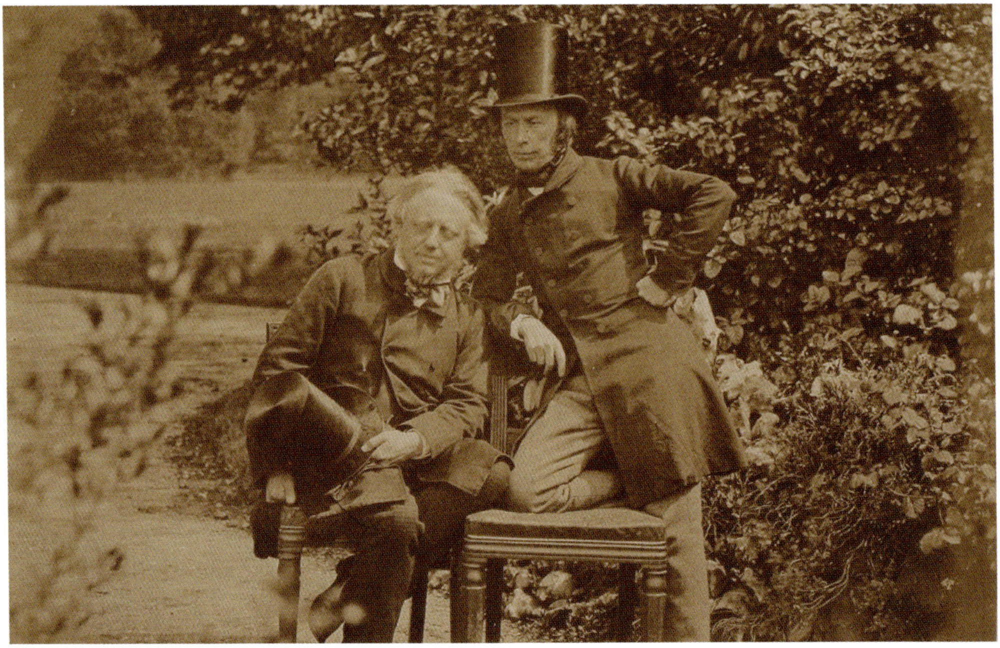

DESIGN PARTNERSHIP

Cole photographed with Richard Redgrave in the gardens of Gore House, probably in the 1860s.

issued a series of pamphlets early in 1853 under the pseudonym of 'Argus', arguing that Marlborough House was a flagrant example of 'taste censorship', 'dictatorship' even, and a breach of the hallowed principle that 'Englishmen know nothing of taste': 'Argus' sensed that the organisers were the kind of people who favoured 'macaroni, wine and frizzled frogs'. Maybe, suggested one newspaper in response, the anonymous pamphleteer had seen one of his own products 'cruelly gibbeted' in the Chamber of Horrors and was getting his own back. Maybe other manufacturers and free traders contributed to the debate. The thing was that several of the exhibits were commercially very successful, however 'unprincipled' they might be from a design point of view. Chintzes and pictorial wallpapers were particularly popular. After ten months perhaps the exhibits looked somewhat dog-eared as well. Unfortunately, there are no illustrations of what the chamber as a whole looked like – or indeed of any of the galleries – until around the time of the move from Marlborough House to South Kensington in 1857, some four years later. There are several watercolours of the Museum's interior dating from the move, showing cluttered display cases and a romantic-style interior.

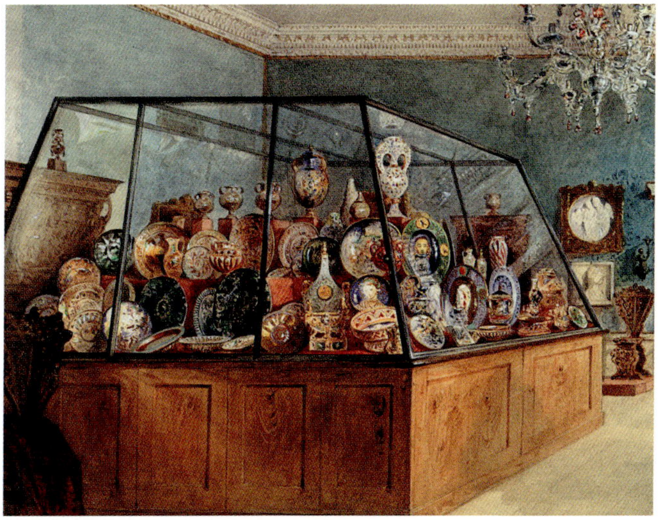

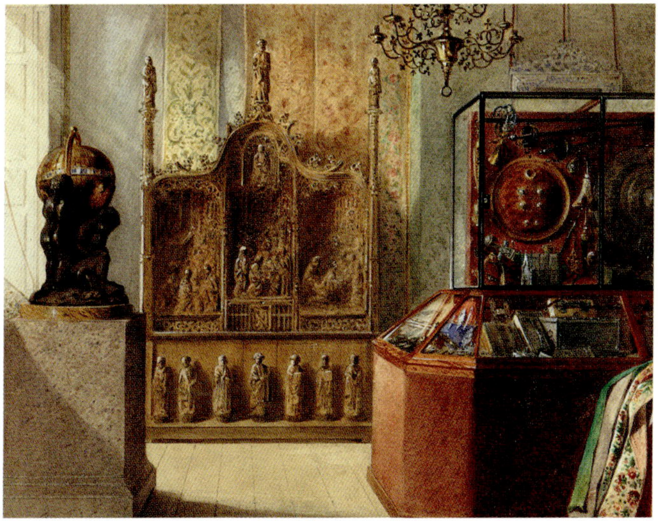

A MUSEUM IN THE MAKING

ABOVE & FOLLOWING PAGES: *Watercolours by William Casey of the interior of the museum at Marlborough House, dating from its impending move to South Kensington in 1857 some four years after the 'Chamber of Horrors' had been closed*

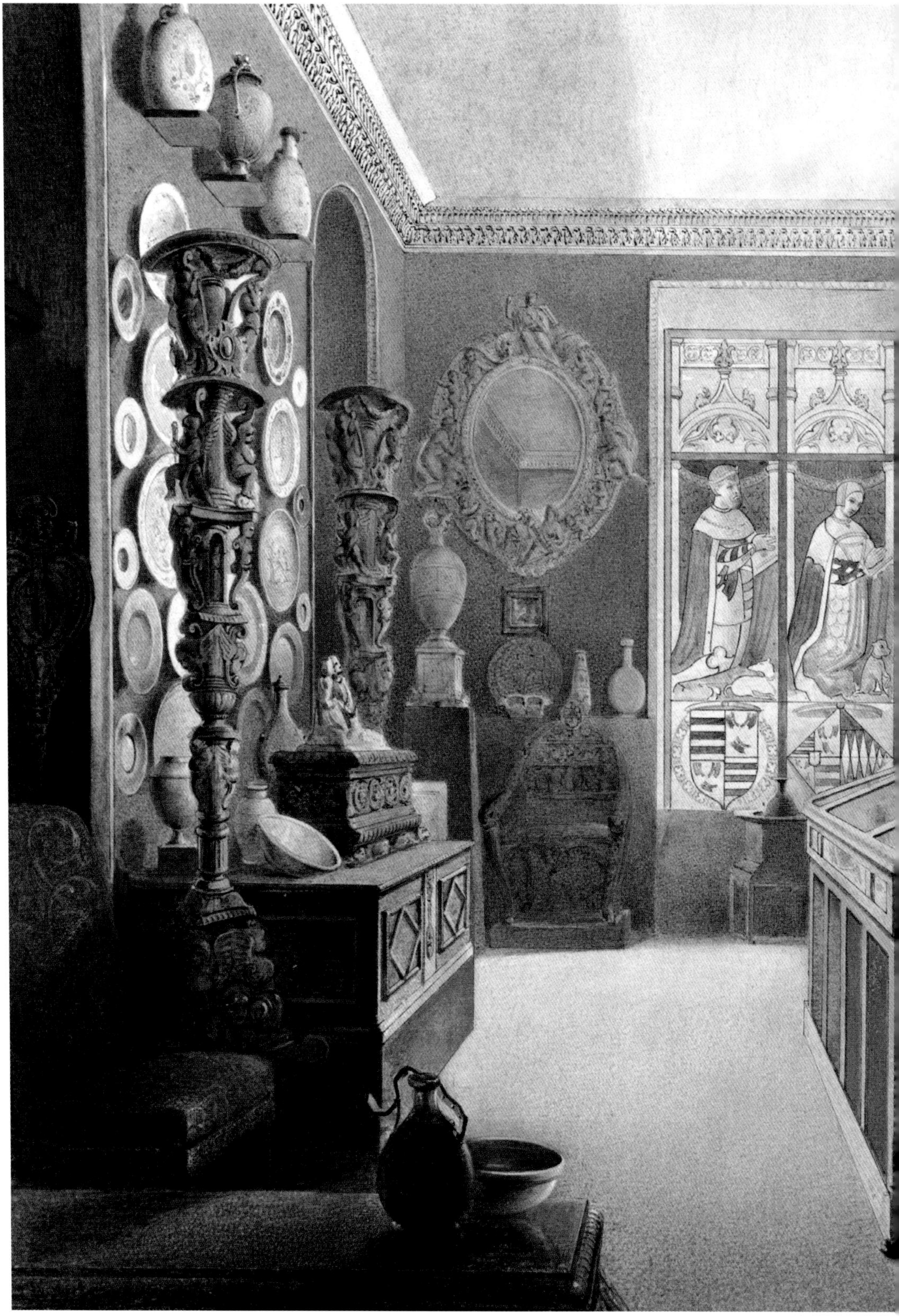

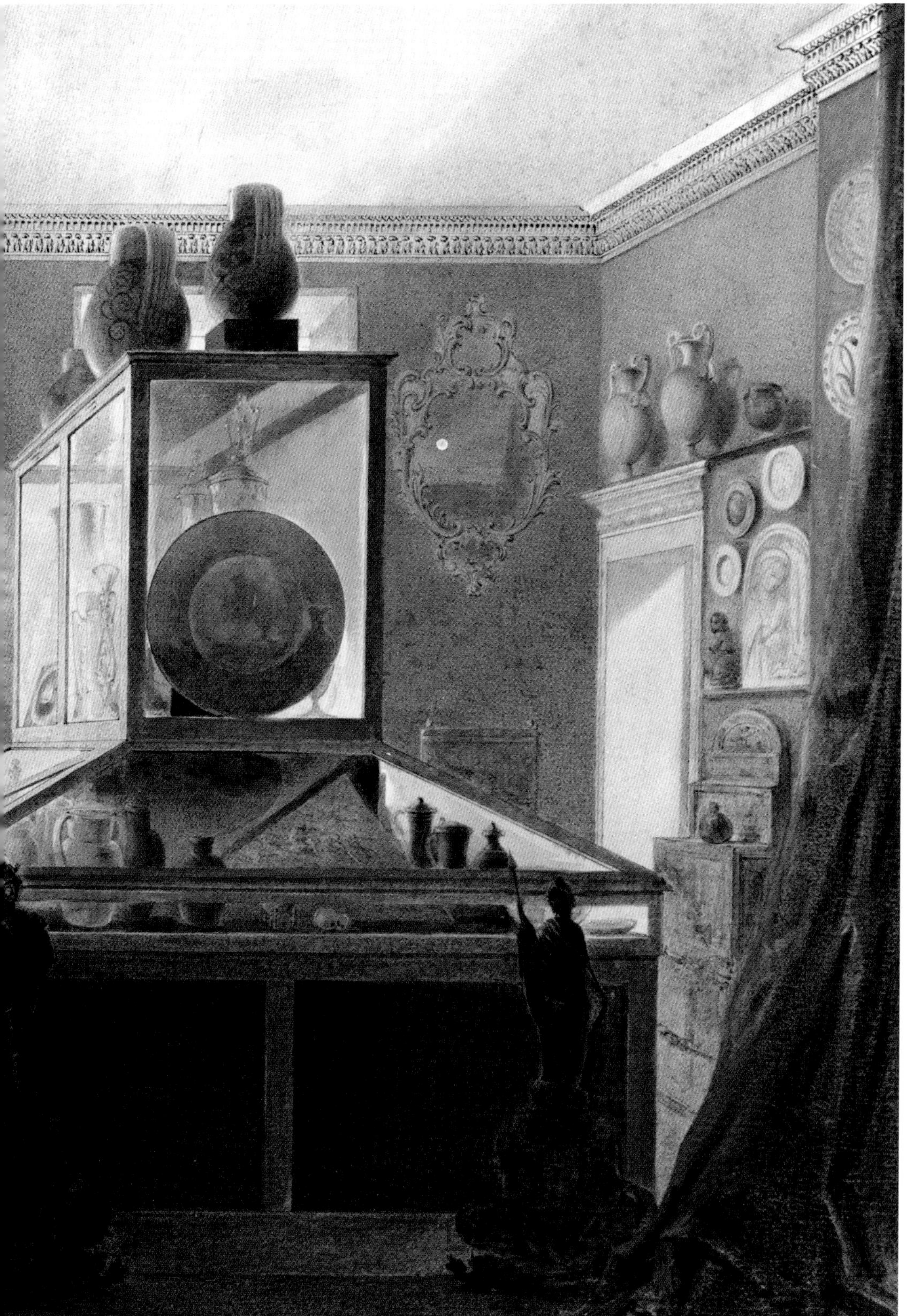

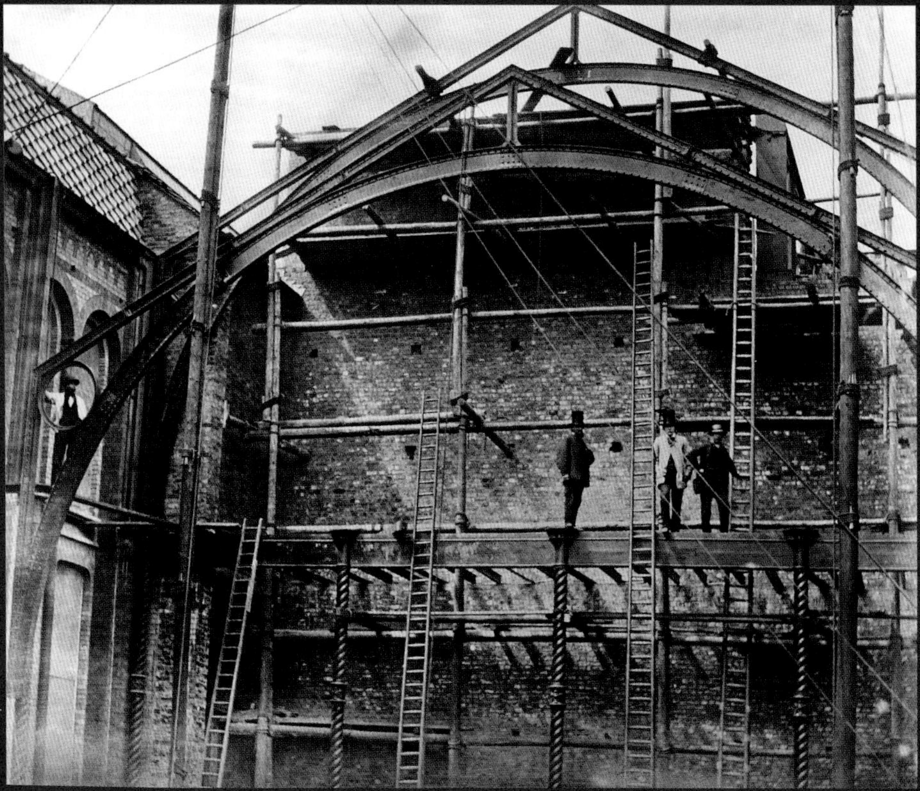

THE NEW MUSEUM EMERGES

Building the South Court, c.1861. The South Court was an iron and glass structure, lavishly decorated with cast and wrought iron work designed by Godfrey Sykes. It featured a series of arcades, deliberately echoing the east wall of the Sheepshanks Gallery, which was incorporated into the Court's interior

A Powerful Antidote to the Gin Palace

In which the Museum of Manufactures evolves, through curatorial selection and the survival of the fittest, into the great Victoria and Albert Museum.

By that time, the original tripartite aims of the Museum – to offer exhibitions and facilities for the benefit of design students, interested members of the manufacturing population and the public-as-consumers – were beginning to fade. This is a story that has often been told.

The Museum of Manufactures became the Museum of Ornamental Art and then the South Kensington Museum, which became less and less interested in specialised design education and contemporary design, more and more in antiquarianism and possession, until in 1880 all the modern objects were finally banished – that was the word they used – banished from the Museum to Bethnal Green – including Henry Cole's tea set, which upset him mightily. He even thought of asking the Museum to give it back. John Charles Robinson – the great Victorian curator and scholar, who founded the Medieval and Renaissance holdings of the Museum, wrote with evident pride at the end of the century – after Cole had gone:

'There was, in truth, little of abiding value in the 1851 exhibition residuum, and the first efforts of the new curator [Robinson himself] were to suppress and eliminate a large proportion of it'.

Contemporary work, or 'the fluctuating styles of the passing hour', as Robinson put it, was out: 'the acknowledged canons and masterpieces of all time' were in.

The typologies that Cole, Redgrave and Jones had used in 1852 to make the exhibitions an active educational experience and avoid accusations of simply accumulating treasure at the public expense – something Cole was very sensitive about – had long gone.

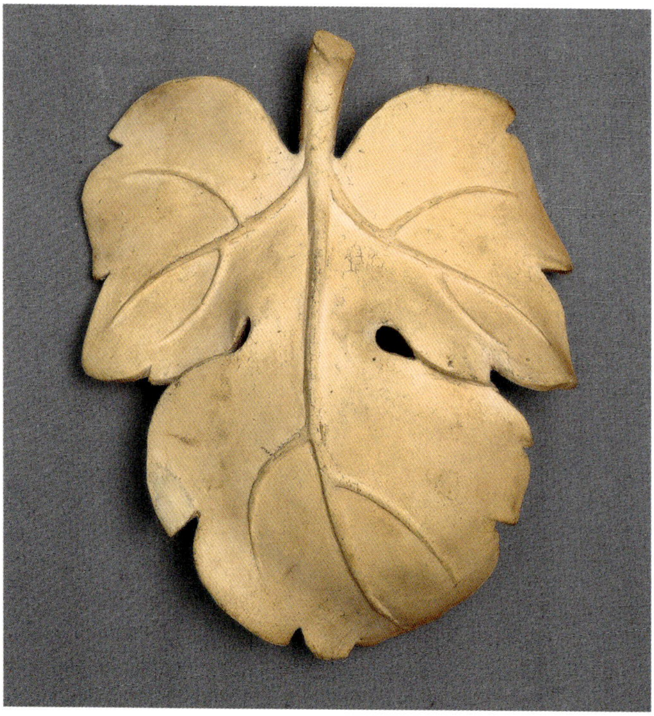

DAVID'S LEAF

A hinged, plaster fig leaf, specially made for Michelangelo's David to accommodate royal visits

As had the critical, didactic stance, which went back at least as far as the *Journal of Design* and its shaming of unprincipled designs before a group of self-appointed experts. The Department of Practical Art became the Department of Science & Art in March 1853. The Schools of Design became the Art Training Schools in the same year. Some of the workshops and practical classes in Textiles, Metalwork, Furniture and Painting on Porcelain (as distinct from the twenty-stage national curriculum in elementary and advanced drawing), workshops which had moved from Somerset House to Marlborough House, did then move on to South Kensington, but within two years they had all been closed.

The rhetoric of stimulating manufactures and sensible consumption through exemplars of good design (old and new, copies and originals), of training members of the manufacturing population in design awareness, and purchasing objects

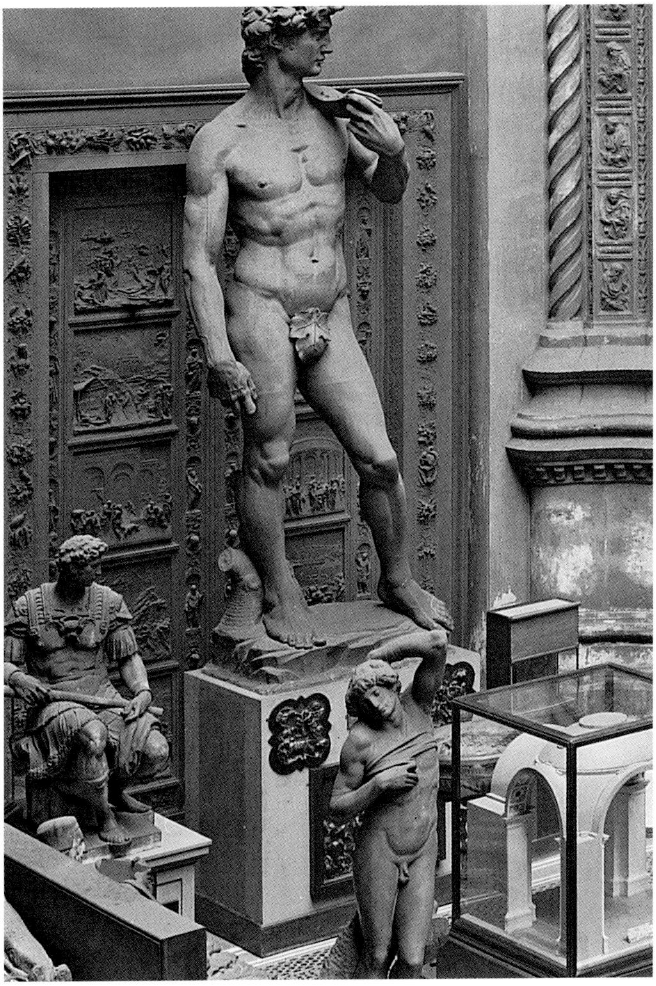

DAVID, READIED FOR ROYALTY

A cast of Michelangelo's David in the cast courts of the V&A, complete with fig leaf. The role of the art school was to teach the grammar, rather than the usage. And to teach it through copying from plaster casts: one wag referred to this system as 'cast-rated'.

or casts to inspire the specialised students, was still useful when pitching for government resources, but from the 1860s onwards it had an increasingly hollow ring to it. Those who have closely studied the accounts of the South Kensington Museum at this time have observed that from then on, most of the money was redirected towards purchases, accumulation and display, and away from the Museum's original educational mission.

'... Museums are antidotes to brutality and vice.'

Cole still kept flying the flag, but even his arguments were beginning to shift their ground: it was now more a question of education in a broader sense, improving national taste, through visits to a 'storehouse' or 'treasury' for public education. 'Museums may furnish a powerful antidote to the gin palace', he wrote in autumn 1857, and the important thing was to arrange the exhibits 'so clearly that they may woo the ignorant to examine them'. He was no longer talking primarily to art students and manufacturers – or even to 'the public' as consumer.

In a famous and often quoted speech about the role of the Museum, which he gave in Birmingham in 1874, he said:

'Schools of Art are there to instruct chiefly the young, but Museums are there to instruct young and old... they are temples where all can worship in harmony; they teach good habits of order, and cleanliness and politeness ... Museums are antidotes to brutality and vice.'

Even though he had moved from targeted didactic instruction to general aesthetic inspiration, he still spoke and wrote with the High Victorian moral certainty he had shown in the original catalogue for Marlborough House in the glory days of 1852.

'By proper arrangements a Museum may be made in the highest degree instructional. If it be connected with lectures, and means are taken to point out its uses and applications, it becomes elevated from being a mere unintelligible lounge for idlers into an impressive schoolroom for everyone.'

One turning-point for Cole was the London International Exhibition of 1861, which had missed its deadline and was rescheduled for 1862 – partly because of the death of Prince Albert. It's as if the London Olympics were to be postponed to 2013. The Exhibition's stated mission – to show how far British manufacturing and education had advanced since 1851 – was bound to lead to disappointment and even disenchantment with the 'South Kensington system', as by then it was known. And to some extent it did. Ten years was much too short a time seriously to take stock. The building, south of the Royal Horticultural Society's Gardens on the Museum's side of the street was controversial, thought to be ugly and featureless. And the layout was far too cluttered this time – with a deep, gloomy colour scheme chosen by Henry Cole himself, unlike Owen Jones's light primary colour-coding for the

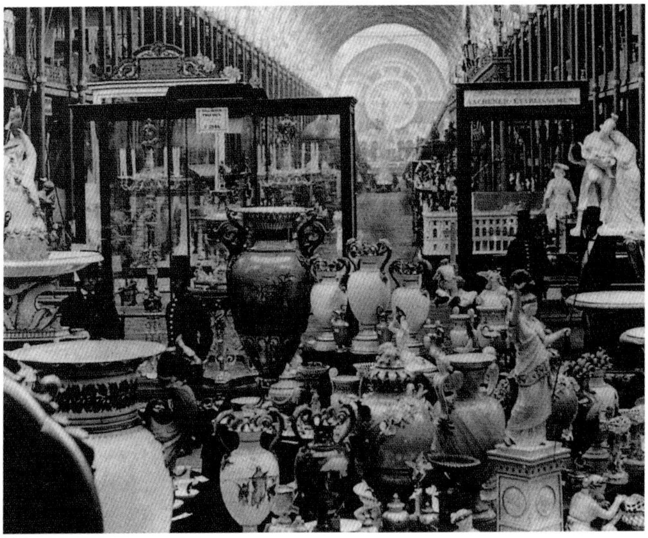

THE GROVES OF BLARNEY

A wildly over-crowded interior from the 1862 Exhibition: 'The Groves of Blarney were order and good taste in comparison'

interior of the Crystal Palace in 1851. A visitor to the opening of the 1862 Exhibition described the entrance hall. The ceremony began with a stirring rendition of the Hallelujah Chorus, but after that it was downhill all the way:

'The Groves of Blarney were order and good taste in comparison with the conglomeration of organs, telescopes, light-houses, fountains, obelisks, pickles, furs, stuffs, porcelain, dolls, rocking-horses, alabasters and [a statue of] Lady Godiva which reduced the nave to a striking similitude of a traveller's description of Hog-Lane, Canton.'

I fear that an ancestor of mine may have contributed to this chaos of sound and vision.[7] One of the organs proudly exhibited in 1862 – and it won an honourable mention – was a large mechanical Orchestrion designed by my great-grandfather on my mother's side Daniel Imhof. It was exhibit No. 3414 in the 'musical instruments' category. Daniel had emigrated from South Germany after the Revolution of 1848 and set up in New Oxford Street a shop and showroom selling clocks, barrel pianos, musical boxes, orchestrions and organs – with his business partner Leopold Mukle. Duplicates of the 1862 orchestrion were available for sale at Imhof's Euterpeon Room. 'The orchestrion', said the handout, 'more durable than any pianoforte or organ, and the most

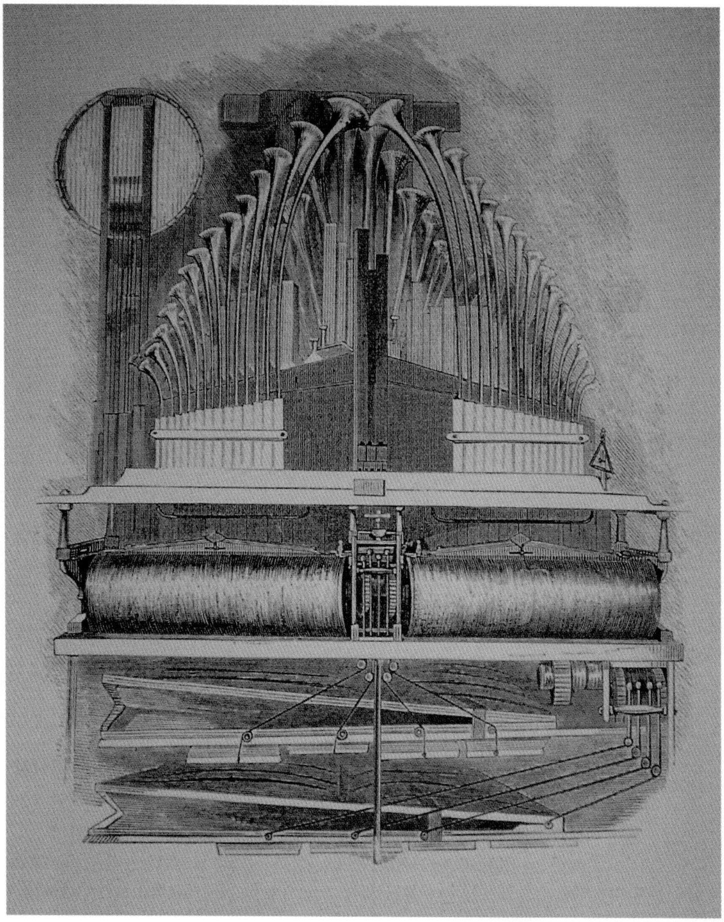

THE ORCHESTRION

A catalogue illustration of the Imhof orchestrion, or 'self-acting organ', exhibited in the London International Exhibition of 1861 that had to be rescheduled for 1862

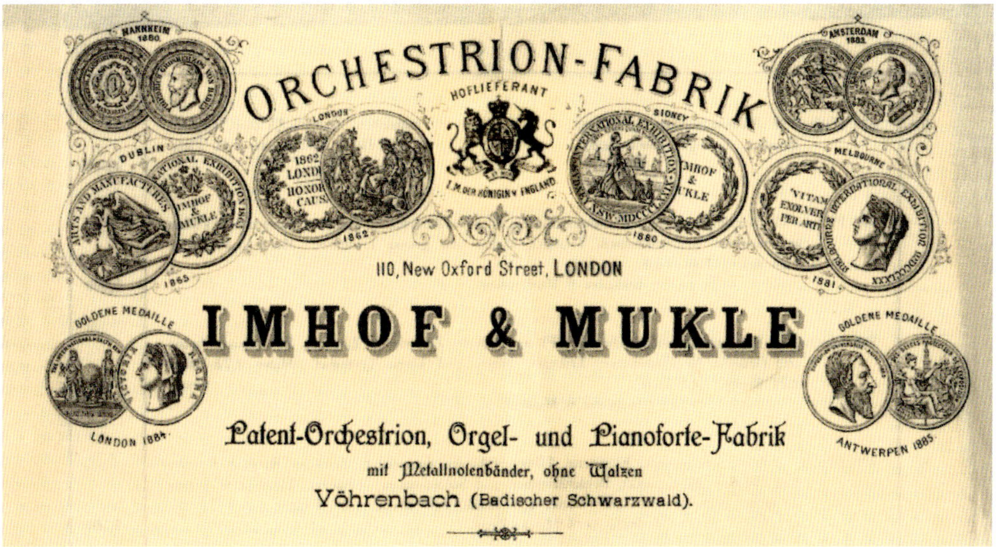

THE MAKERS

Headed notepaper of the Imhof and Mukle Shop and showroom at 110, New Oxford Street

perfect scale to produce varieties of tone and orchestral effects. The orchestrion is capable of giving expression to the music played, with greater ease and precision than any other instrument ever made. [All the music is arranged by Daniel Imhof himself]. Only two winding places! An abundant supply of wind! A tempo regulator! The mechanisms of the orchestrion will be found to work without the slightest noise, and are guaranteed to remain so'.

I have heard a similar model in action – and the *mechanism* may be quiet, but the noise it makes when wound up is indescribable. It must have blasted the other exhibits to kingdom come.

The main point is that by 1862 the tide was definitely turning , and one designer who deeply regretted the passing of the 'Chamber of Horrors' approach was Christopher Dresser, who had been a scholar at the Government School of Design at precisely the same time as the School moved from Somerset House to Marlborough House, in 1852. He studied textile fabrics and painting in the practical workshops, became a tutor and went on to become Britain's foremost industrial designer. Dresser wrote in retrospect about the closing of the False Principles Gallery:

'This I have never ceased to regret ... [there were] scissors formed as birds, which separated into halves

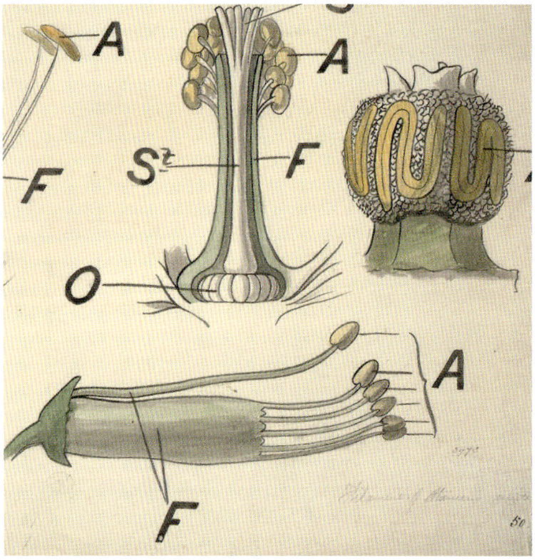

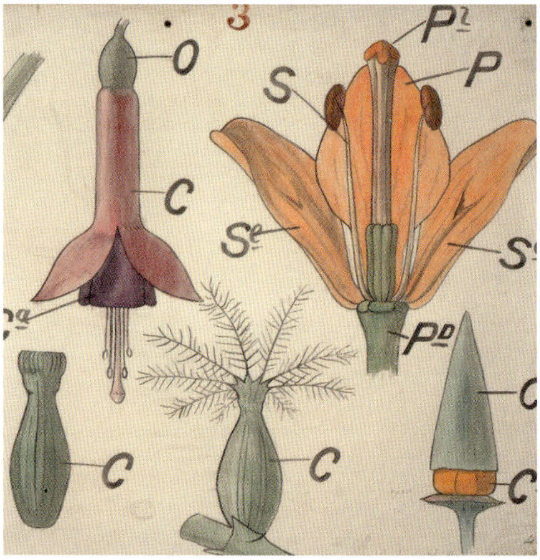

DRAWINGS BY DRESSER

Botanical drawings by Dresser, which he used as visual aids as a student teacher in the early 1850s

every time the scissors were opened; candle-sticks formed as human beings ... plaid fabrics bearing check patterns so large that it almost required two persons to wear the same pattern in order that the whole design be seen ... and other absurdities equally offensive to good taste'.

These, he said, were very useful educational devices, and indeed Dresser himself was to use them as teaching props, when he worked as a tutorial assistant at the Government Schools – and to devote much thought to the principles of decorative design; principles of use mainly. Some of the boards from Marlborough House were in fact still being used for teaching in the Schools until the 1890s. Design practitioners seem to have been more in favour of the Chamber – with its explicit criteria of judgement – than curators, manufacturers and free traders.

On the other hand, one of the sternest and most consistent critics of the Marlborough House Doctrine *and* of 'the South Kensington system' was John Ruskin, a writer whose work on education Henry Cole knew well. Over Christmas 1853, a few months after the Chamber of Horrors had closed, Cole was reading Ruskin on education at home. And he was soon to visit St Mark's Square in Venice, with a copy of Ruskin's *Stones of Venice* to hand.

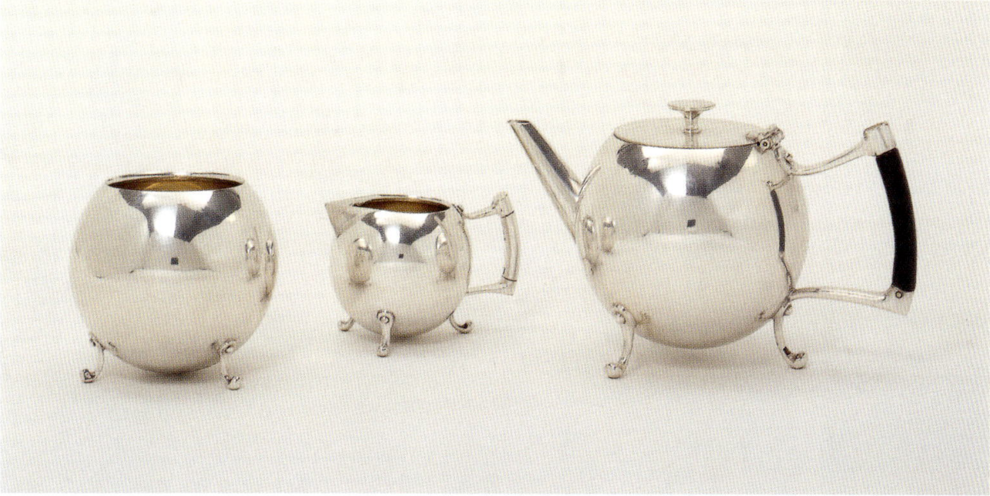

A DRESSER DESIGN

The clean lines of an electroplated tea set, designed by Christopher Dresser

In the *Journal of Design* [for October 1849], Henry Cole had reviewed *The Seven Lamps of Architecture* and sent a copy to Ruskin, in the hope he might contribute to the magazine. But Ruskin – understandably – declined. Because Cole wrote this:

'Instead of boldly recognising the tendencies of the [modern] age, which are inevitable, perceiving the wide distribution of certain kinds of art, and the positive good that is in this … he either puts up his back against their further development, or would attempt to bring back the work of art to what its course of action was four centuries ago! As easy a thing as to put the world itself back.'

'… scissors formed as birds … ; candle-sticks formed as human beings … plaid fabrics bearing check patterns so large that it almost required two persons to wear the same pattern in order that the whole design be seen … and other absurdities equally offensive to good taste'

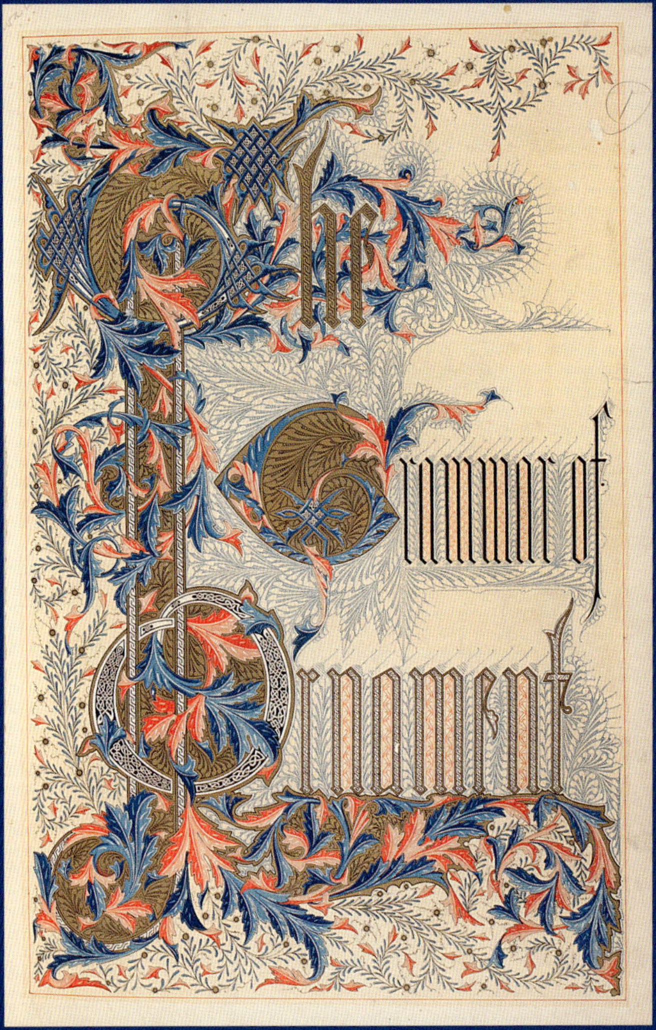

THE HEAD: LEARNING GRAMMAR

The title page of Owen Jones' famous Grammar of Ornament, *1856*

Head, Heart & Hand

In which John Ruskin helps us through the subsequent story of art and design education in South Kensington and beyond, and we are reunited with Jim.

Cole and Ruskin have often been seen as at opposite ends of the educational spectrum: the rule-bound and the imaginative; the utilitarian and the romantic; the committee man and the free-floating intellectual. This does less than justice to both men. But a little later on, and in reaction against teaching by true and false principles, John Ruskin famously said during a Manchester lecture:

'The education of a young artist should always be a matter of the *head* and *heart* and *hand* going together.'

'... Art must always be produced by the subtlest of all machines, which is the human hand. No machine yet contrived or hereafter contrivable, will ever equal the fine machinery of the human fingers. Thoroughly perfect art is that which proceeds from the heart, which involves all the noble emotions; associates these with the head, yet as inferior to the heart; and the hand, yet as inferior to the heart and head; and thus brings out the whole man'.[8]

The head, the heart and the hand – for me, this provides an elegant way of summarising the whole subsequent history of art and design education.[9] First, the 'head' period of Victorian times, when design was thought to be a kind of language – Cole in fact referred to 'drawing as a second language' – a language with its principles, its grammars and its rules. The role of the art school was to teach the grammar, rather than the usage. And to teach it through copying from plaster casts: one wag referred to this system as 'cast-rated'. It's easy to mock this approach – apart from anything else, to mock its prudery. But from an intellectual point of view, it was a world-beater. Christopher Dresser, the world's first industrial designer

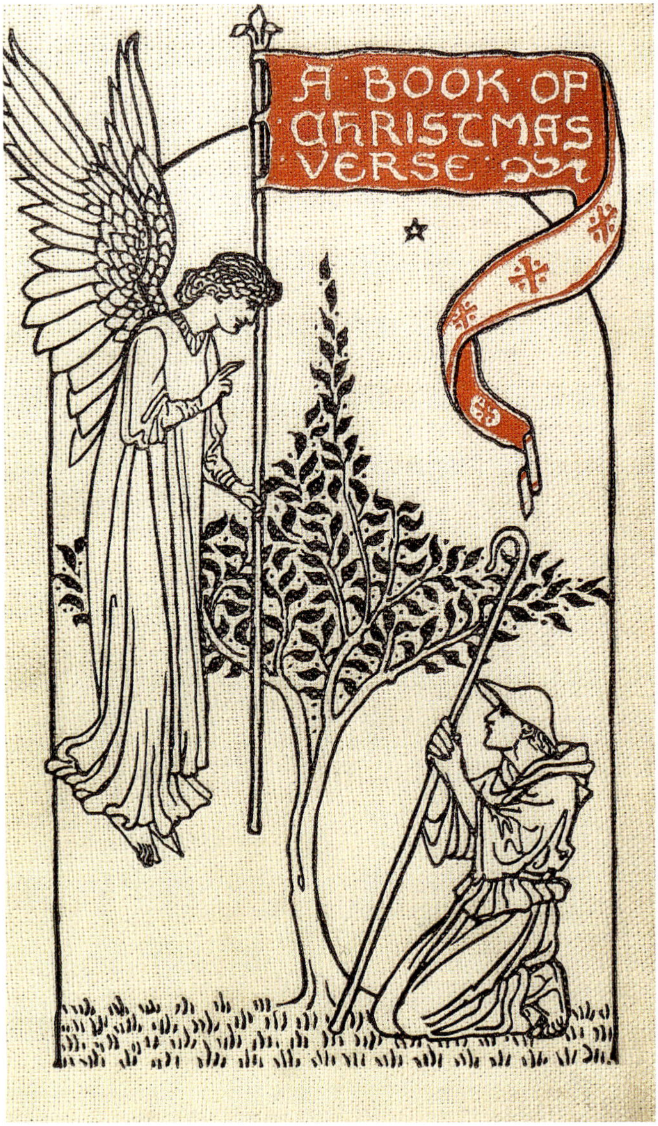

CHRISTMAS VERSE

A binding designed by the designer and artist Walter Crane, who was Principal of the Royal College of Art for just one year, 1898–99 on the principles of design and the symmetry of natural forms; Owen Jones on the grammar of ornament; T H Huxley on art botany; Gottfried Semper on the formal components of style; the first design journal or style magazine in history – and so on. South Kensington was in those days the world centre for theorising design and manufacture, at the hub of a genuinely national system. With the new interest in design databases and systematic design methods, this philosophy is in fact making a comeback.

The 'head' period dates from a time when educational reformers were struggling to create schools of design which were distinct from art academies, universities and – the closest model – Mechanics' Institutes. The 'hand' period of Edwardian times, up to the 1930s, in reaction against the constraints of the South Kensington system, instead emphasised usage, or making and doing. To understand design you had first of all to understand how it was produced – so, under the delayed influence of the Arts and Crafts Movement, there would be a new emphasis on workshops and the basic craft technologies. W R Lethaby – the very first Professor of Ornament and Design in Britain – said that the following words should be inscribed in the finest lettering over the front door of every art and design college: 'no art that is only one person deep can be very good art'.

The point was to belong to a tradition of designing and making, and to work from within that tradition. In rare cases, Lethaby added, students would be able to stand on the shoulders of the previous generation, but they should *never* be permitted to jump off those shoulders. And their work should be a reaction against the shoddiness of the high street, just like their forebears though for very different reasons.

Again, let us look at the thinking behind *this* philosophy of design education, say in the 1910s. We have C R Ashbee on craft apprenticeships and art schools; Lethaby on outline, colour, shapes and the role of making; the *Artistic Crafts* series of technical handbooks, most of them written by teaching staff at the Royal College of Art (which adopted the name in 1896, three years before the South Kensington Museum became the Victoria and Albert Museum).

Ruskin's complaint about 'the hand' was that if over-emphasised, this approach could neglect the head and the heart. But with today's concerns about the environment, the social responsibilities of the artist and designer, and the contemporary role of the crafts in both art *and* design, this too, has made a comeback. By the post-war period, it was often being said that *this* tradition wasn't giving the students enough opportunities to *express* their own ideas and concepts – and it could not hope to touch the real issues of the modern world. It was one thing to half educate students by mistake: it was quite another to half educate them deliberately.

So it was generally agreed that the education of the designer should involve much more heart – as well as head and hand – with an emphasis on ideas and education rather than techniques and training. Heart, not at all in the sense of sentimentality, but in the sense of having one's finger on the pulse of what is going on in contemporary culture and the creative industries and caring about them. Heart in the sense of investing the work with emotion. Today is in some ways an era of the convergence of all these traditions – a thoughtful attitude towards design, an understanding through experience of materials and techniques, and – for the first time ever – a sense that art and design education really is in the vanguard, a stimulus to the worlds which surround it. And there are many other convergences at work today, in the era described by David Harvey in his book *The Condition of Postmodernity*:

The relatively stable aesthetic of the era of Henry Ford and modernism, he writes, the era of fixities and certainties, 'has given way to all the ferment, instability and fleeting qualities of a post-modern aesthetic that celebrates difference, ephemerality, spectacle, simulation, fashion and the commodification of cultural forms'.

In such an era, the keynotes have to be interdisciplinarity – for much of the most interesting work emerges from the spaces between disciplines, the cracks in the floorboards – and design with attitude.

The Museum, as we've seen, started life as a radical and controversial educational experiment. What should it make of this post-modern world, from the educational point of view? Well, you need the space to exercise the head, the hand and the heart – space to think, to make art, space to be fired up. You need a space which combines areas for discussions, with workshops and visual presentations, something like parts of Marlborough House in 1852 where there was the lecture room (the ex-kitchen) some classrooms, and the technical studios, all next to each other. Now that 'taste' has become a sociological or psychological concept rather than a scientific principle, you need space to think about art and identity, cultures rather than culture, why we consume the things we do. Post-Marx, Freud and Feminism, things look a little different. And you need a place to make work. In short, you need a space rather like the Sackler Centre – the largest dedicated educational centre this Museum has ever had. A centre – as the subtitle goes – for creative practice.

'Thoroughly perfect art is that which proceeds from the heart, which involves all the noble emotions; associates these with the head, yet as inferior to the heart; and the hand, yet as inferior to the heart and head; and thus brings out the whole man'

When first I became a Professor at the Royal College of Art – a university institution which is the direct descendant of the Government Schools of Design – Sir Roy Strong was kind enough to introduce my inaugural lecture. This was when I became directly involved in the governance

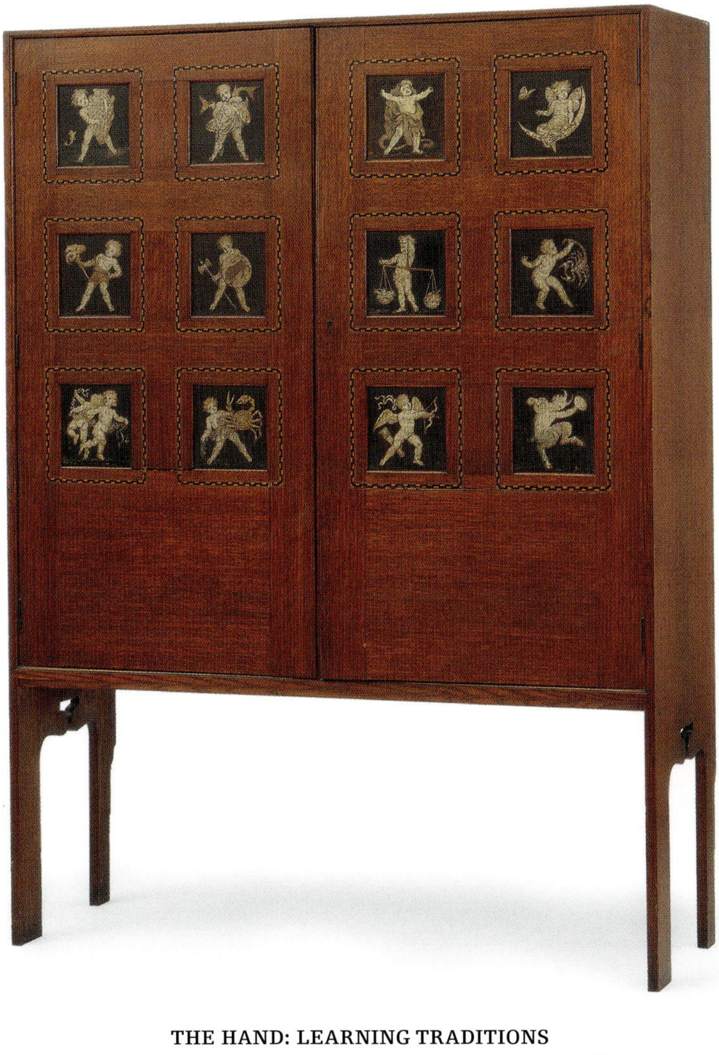

THE HAND: LEARNING TRADITIONS

An embroidery cabinet, decorated with signs of the zodiac and designed by Lewis Foreman Day in the 1880s. Day taught at the Royal College of Art, contributed to a report on the College's performance, and was an articulate champion of the Arts and Crafts philosophy in art education – the tradition of the hand.'

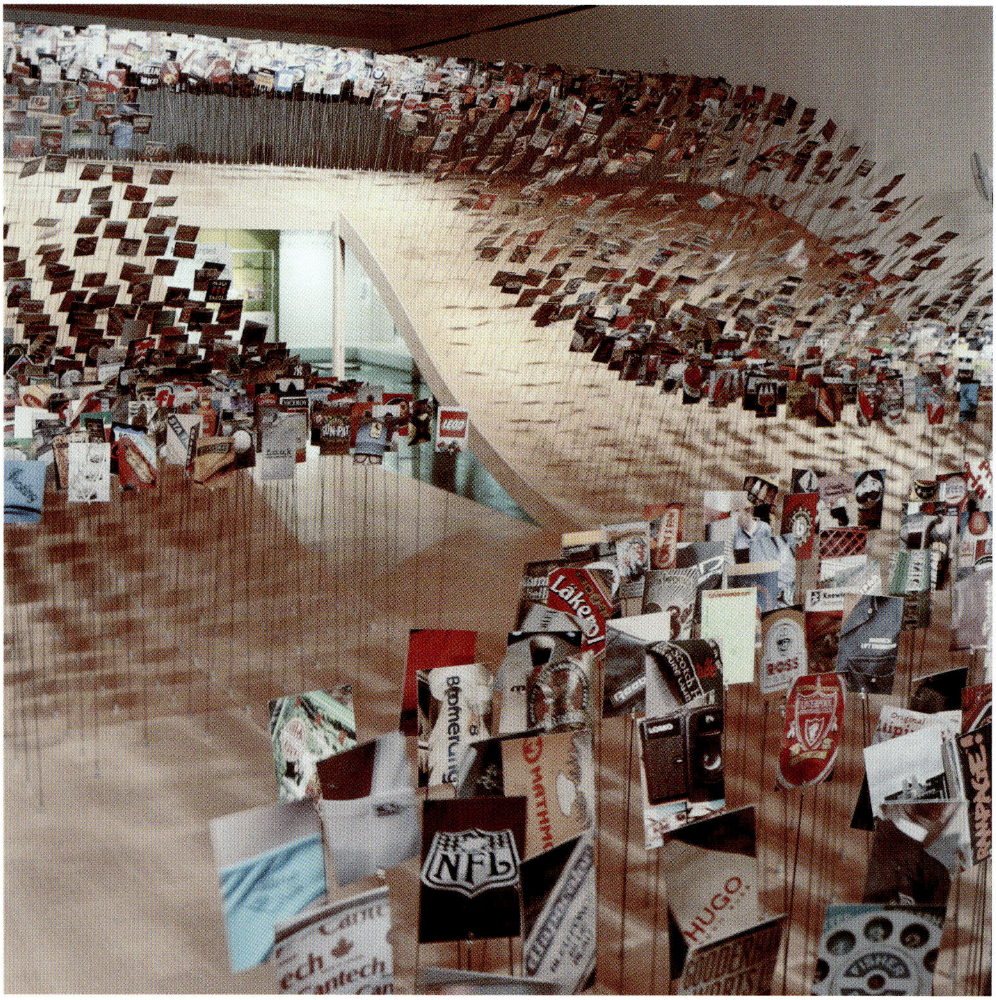

THE HEART: LEARNING EXPRESSION

A field of brands installed and designed by Tom Heatherwick for the V&A exhibition brand.new; *Heatherwick was a student at the RCA from 1992 to 1994.*

of the V&A. I vividly remember one conversation I had with him around that time – in 1980, it was. Roy had said that the RCA grew from within the Victoria and Albert Museum – so we shared a common heritage. I replied that the second statement was correct, but, as for the first, it was actually the other way round: the Victoria and Albert Museum started life as the visual aids department of the Government School of Design: the collection grew out of the plaster casts acquired for the students to copy; the library grew out of the texts on design intended for the students and the branch schools; the displays at Marlborough House were predominantly aimed at the students – on Wednesdays to Saturdays, anyway; the lecture theatre was originally built over the entrance at the time, partly for the thousands of students in the national system; and above all, the founding mission of the Museum was an unashamedly educational mission. Roy gladly acknowledged the point. Now, I'm recalling this not to present myself as the Emperor of Arizona, and lay claim to whole swathes of the Museum in the name of the College – though that would be nice – but to finish on just how central – uniquely central – education was in the foundation of this great institution.

In the early 1980s, at the time of my conversation with Roy, the relationship between College and Museum was at a very low ebb – symbolised by the nailing up of the shared door between them and then the move of the College out of the South Kensington Museum buildings where it had been since the 1870s to the other end of the street. Since then, I've spent a lot of my professional career – through the joint courses, exhibitions, events and publications, and through my long membership of the Trustees – building bridges between the two institutions and reminding both of their shared family history and resemblances, to the point where they are now, or should I say once again, very close indeed.

A confession. Henry Cole, especially the Henry Cole of the 1840s and 1850s, is one of my heroes – in fact I have the *Vanity Fair* picture of him hanging above my desk in Bath. I think history tends not to be very kind to people like Henry. Of course, we've moved on from the Chamber of Horrors – although its explicit criteria of judgement and its very public critical stance on design and consumption are still challenging. But his belief in Albertopolis – or Coleville as I prefer to call it: not Coketown but Coleville – the bringing together on one street of art, design and science; design and technology; fine and applied art; visual art and music; specialised students and the general public; this belief I profoundly share. And I share his conviction that the heart of this museum lies in education, research and engagement with contemporary design: all this in relation to, and in addition to, its responsibilities to history. He used all the media available in *his* day to put the message across, was fascinated by the latest technologies – in his case, photography, electroplating, mechanical reproduction – and had a real flair for lobbying in the right places.

Cole – like me –was awarded the Albert Medal by what is now the Royal Society of Arts for services to design. He was on every committee going, not because he collected committees but because he found them a useful way

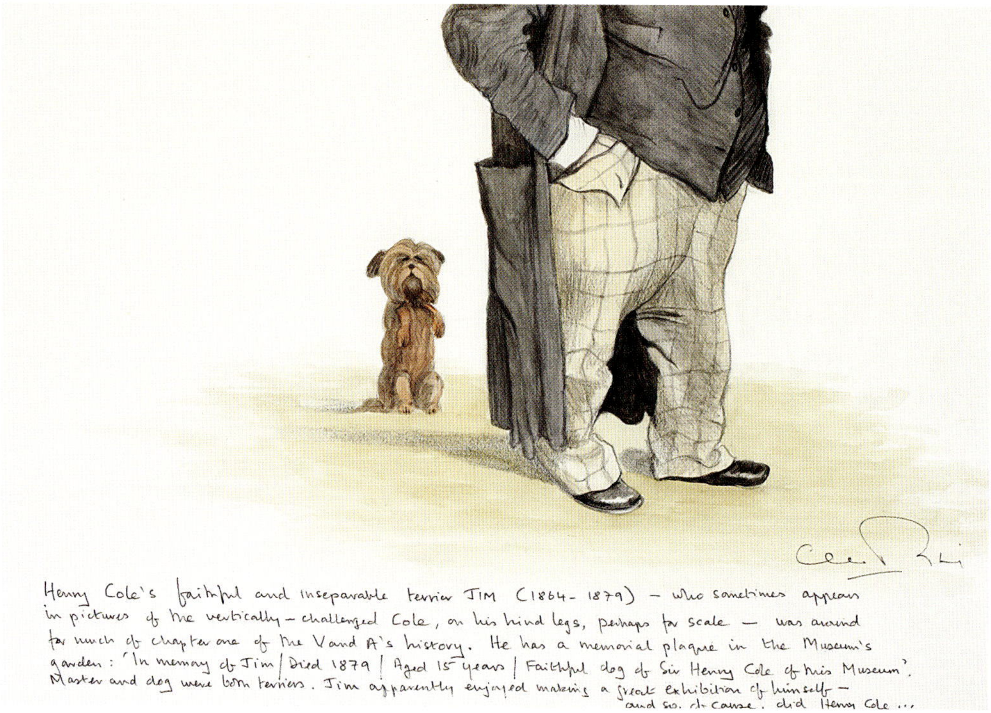

MAN AND DOG

The author's watercolour created for the V&A's 150th anniversary album

of getting things done in the arts. In fact, he could be quite cynical about committees at times, particularly when they didn't achieve what he wanted. He was a philosophical radical in his youth – like most of the great and the good who were behind the Government School and Museum – and retained a strong social conscience throughout his career. He tended to see the glass as half-full – as in 'Felix Summerly'.

On his family holidays, he was always writing lectures, speeches and books, and visiting museums and cultural institutions. He had a prodigious amount of energy. I deeply admire all this and – for better or worse – I like to think it in some ways resembles my own approach to life. He should have been given a knighthood in 1851, inside the Crystal Palace, but he had to wait another 24 years for that – partly one suspects because he'd rubbed so many people up the wrong way, was so forceful and argumentative and had such a short fuse. He once referred to a lecturer at one of the branch art schools as 'like an untamed Newfoundland dog', which wasn't intended as a compliment. Because *he*, of course, was a terrier. As

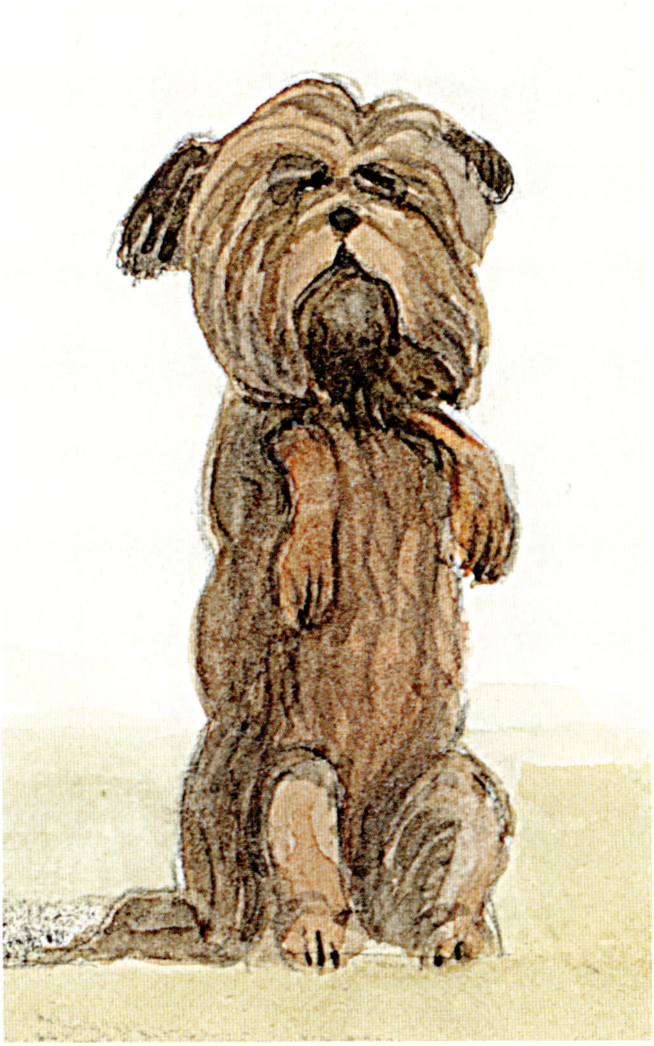

JUST JIM

Henry Cole's terrier Jim, detail of the watercolour shown on the opposite page

Lyon Playfair – who worked closely with Cole on the Great Exhibition – once said:

'He was constantly misjudged because his modes of work were not always on the surface. If he came to an obstacle, it was his delight to tunnel under it in secret, and unexpectedly come out at the other side'.

Or to put it another way, as another Victorian contemporary did:

'[He had] a dogged inventive genius which knew how to turn difficulties into stepping stones to success, and to wear out stolid opposition by vivacious pertinacity'.

Which perhaps explains why Henry Cole and Jim had so much in common. I congratulate the V&A on picking up the gauntlet thrown down by Henry Cole in 1853 – 155 years ago – and for doing this in a way which is so much more suited to the modern world.

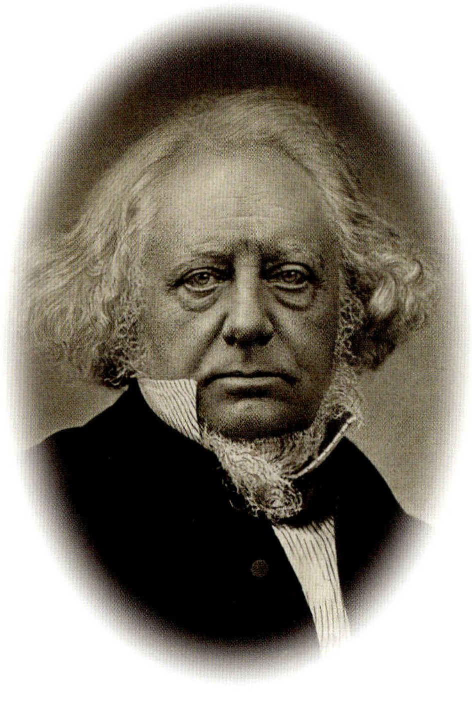

'He was constantly misjudged because his modes of work were not always on the surface. If he came to an obstacle, it was his delight to tunnel under it in secret, and unexpectedly come out at the other side'

List of Illustrations

2 V&A: 355 - 1886 – Portrait of Henry Cole by A.J.Melhuish, 1870. Photograph

6 Sir Henry Cole and Richard Redgrave in the garden at Gore House; attributed to Charles Thurston Thompson (1816 - 68); 1854. Albumen print (detail)

8 V&A: E.2178 - 1932 – Cartoon for Vanity Fair – Sir Henry Cole by James Tissot (1836 - 1902); French; August 1871. Colour lithograph

10 V&A: AL 7851 – Prince Albert Inspecting the Great Exhibition Memorial; by Anthony Stannus; English; 1861. Watercolour, 26.8 x 36.7 cm

12 V&A: E.478:3 - 2008 – Page of V&A 150th anniversary album. Professor Sir Christopher Frayling, 'Henry Cole's faithful and inseparable terrier Jim', 2007 (detail)

14 V&A: 26471:4 – Jim at Broadstairs by Sir Henry Cole; etching of Henry Cole's dog. 1864. The print is dedicated to Lord Hawarden

15 Photograph V&A Images 2009

16 V&A: E.561 - 1980 – Wallpaper; Unknown; England; *c.* 1853. Colour print from wood block, possibly with some machine printing (detail)

22 V&A neg No.71821 – Handbill announcing opening of museum at Marlborough House, 1852, with corrections by Henry Cole

24 NAL: 236.C.17 – Illustration of Marlborough House published within John Weale's guide book *London Exhibited* in 1851

25 NAL: PP.10 – *Illustrated London News*; 1843, vol.2, p 375; School of Design

26 NAL: 52.D.68 – The General Principals of Decorative Art; *from Principles of Decorative Art, Science & Art Dept.* Published by Chapman & Hall, London; 1853

28 NAL: 602.AD – From a lithographic plan printed by Day & Son, included in the *First Report of the Department of Practical Art,* 1853

30 V&A: E.558 - 1980 – Wallpaper: Perspective views of a railway station; colour print from wood blocks, on paper; produced by Potters of Darwen; English (Lancashire); *c.* 1853. (detail)

31 V&A: W.6 - 1920 – Tray; papier-mâché with picture of a huntsman & a cook; English; *c.* 1840

32 V&A: T.10 - 1933 – Furnishing Fabric; glazed-printed cotton with floral pattern of roses & budleia; English (Lancashire); *c.* 1850

35 V&A: T.11 - 1933 – Furnishing fabric; roller printed and glazed cotton; possibly Jackson & Graham; English (Lancashire); *c.* 1850

36 V&A: T.8 - 1933 – Block-printed chintz; Hollyhock; labelled False Principles No.10, Imitation of Nature; *c.* 1850

37 V&A: T.6 - 1933 – Furnishing fabric; False Principles No.16; roller printed & glazed cotton; English (Lancashire); *c.* 1850

39 V&A: E.558 - 1980 – Wallpaper: Perspective views of a railway station; colour print from wood blocks, on paper; produced by Potters of Darwen; English (Darwen, Lancashire); *c.* 1853.

40 V&A: E.158 - 1934 – Colour machine print on paper; Heywood, Higginbottom & Smith, Manchester 1853 - 55

41 V&A: E.559 - 1980 – Wallpaper; Perspective representations of architecture; colour print from wood blocks, on paper; unknown maker; English; *c.* 1853

42 NAL: 86.MM.29 – Illustration of modern gothic wallpaper from Pugin's *True Principles of Pointed or Christian Architecture*; London : J. Weale, 1841

43 V&A: E.562 - 1980 – Wallpaper; colour print from wood block, possibly with some machine printing; unknown manufacture; England, *c.* 1853

44 V&A: E.561 - 1980 – Wallpaper; Colour print from wood block, possibly with some machine printing.; unknown manufacture; England; *c.* 1853

45 V&A: E.563 - 1980 – Wallpaper; paper; – False Principles No. 36a, unknown; English; *c.* 1851

List of Illustrations

49 *False principles in decoration.* A catalogue of the Museum of Ornamental Art at Marlborough House, Pall Mall: for the use of studentsandmanufacturers, and the public.5th ed.

50 V&A: W.6 - 1920 – Tray; papier-mâché with picture of a huntsman & a cook; English; *c.* 1840

51 V&A: C.629 - 1921 – Bread Plate; transfer–printed earthenware; designed by J. Austin & H. Warren; made by F & R Pratt & Co.; English (Fenton, Staffordshire); 1851

52 V&A: M.20 - 1974 – Gas jet Lamp; gilt brass & glass; front view; made by R.W. Winfield; English (Birmingham); Marks for 1848

53 V&A: M.19 - 1974 – Curtain Bracket; gilt brass & white glass; English; *c.* 1848

54 V&A: M.58 - 2000 – Candlestick; electroplated nickel silver; English; *c.* 1852

56 V&A: 2742 - 1901, 2744 - 1901, 2744A - 1901, 2741 - 1901, 2741A - 1901, 2743 - 1901, 2743A - 1901 – The Henry Cole Tea Service – two cups and saucers, milk jug & teapot; cream earthenware; designed by Henry Cole (1808 - 82); made by Minton, Felix Summerly's Art Manufactures; English; 1844 - 46

58 V&A: 540 - 1855 – Jug; Coach & Railway; Designed by H.J.Townsend; Earthenware (Minton); *c.* 1847

59 V&A: 371 - 1865 – Christening Mug with guardian angels; silver, embossed & chased; designed by Richard Redgrave (1804 - 88) for Felix Summerly's Art Manufacture; Manufactured by Harry Emanuel; English; 1865

60, 61, 62 and 63 V&A: PH.835:85 - 1987 and non-accessioned – Shere cottage; Mary, Tishie & Hennie; Albumen print; by Henry Cole; English; 1856

64 V&A: 161 - 1865 – mounted in metal; designed by Richard Redgrave (1804 - 88); English; for Felix Summerlys; made by Wedgwood & Sons; designed 1848; made 1865

65 V&A: 4503 - 1901 – Well Spring Carafe; glass, enamel, painted; designed by Richard Redgrave (1804 - 88); English (Stangate Glassworks, Lambeth, London); made for Felix Summerly's Art Manufactures; 1847 - 51

66 V&A: E.110 - 1939 – 'Lismore' wallpaper: designed by A.W.N.Pugin (1812 - 52)

67 V&A: D.699 - 1908 – Tile design for The Houses of Parliament by A.W.N. Pugin (1812 - 52); English; 1852

68 Henry Cole & Richard Redgrave in the garden at Gore House; attributed to Charles Thurston Thompson (1816 - 68); U.K.; 1854. Albumen print

69, 70 and 71 V&A: AL.7279, AL 7280 – Interiors of Marlborough House by William Casey (1835 - 70); English; 1856. Watercolour

72 V&A: (number unknown): Building the South Court about 1861; photograph

74, 75 Plaster casts of David (and fig leaf) after the marble original by Michelangelo (1475 - 1564) in the Accademia di Belle Arti, Florence, *c.* 1857

77 Photograph (source unknown): the 1862 International Exhibition held in London

78, 79 Courtesy of the Royal Commission for the Exhibition of 1851

81 V&A: CIRC.279 - 1961 – Teapot, milk jug and sugar bowl; electroplated nickel silver and wood; designed by Christopher Dresser; made by James Dixon & Sons; English (Sheffield); 1880

82 The Grammar of Ornament; by Owen Jones; illustrated by examples from various styles of ornament. One hundred folio plates drawn on stone by F. Bedford and printed in colours by Day and Son. Volume 1, 1856

84 NAL: G.29.K.5 – *A Book of Christmas Verse* (London, 1895), selected by H.C. Beeching with ten designs by Walter Crane

87 V&A: CIRC.349:1 - 1955 – Cabinet; oak inlaid with ebony and satinwood; designed by Lewis Foreman Day; made by George McCulloch; English; 1888

88 Installation shot of the *brand.new* exhibition at the V&A in October 2000

90, 91 V&A: E.478:3 - 2008 – Page of V&A 150th anniversary album. Professor Sir Christopher Frayling, 'Henry Cole's faithful and inseparable terrier Jim', 2007

Notes

1 This lecture was given on 30 October 2008 as the first Henry Cole Lecture, in the Sackler Centre of the Victoria and Albert Museum. It owes much to the key studies of the origins of the V&A. These include:

John Physick: *The Victoria and Albert Museum – the history of its building* (Phaidon Christie's, 1982, especially chapters 1 and 2, pp. 13 - 32)

Malcolm Baker and Brenda Richardson (ed): *A Grand Design* (V&A, 1997 especially the sections on the Great Exhibition and the Museum's educational role, pp. 79 - 147)

Anthony Burton: *Vision and Accident – the story of the Victoria and Albert Museum* (V&A, 1999, especially chapters 2 - 5, pp. 26 - 92)

Elizabeth Bonython and Anthony Burton: *The Great Exhibitor – the life and work of Henry Cole* (V&A, 2003)

Lara Kriegel: *Grand Designs – Labor, Empire and the Museum in Victorian Culture* (Duke University Press, 2007, especially chapters 3 and 4, pp. 86 - 159)

2 See Col. W. N. Hutchinson: *Dog Breaking – the most expeditious, certain and easy method...* (3rd edition, John Murray, 1856) and on Hutchinson's contribution:

Graham Cox: 'Teaching a new dog old tricks' (*The Shooting Gazette*, June/July, 1991)

3 On Charles Dickens and Henry Cole, see references in:

Bonython and Burton, *op cit*

K J Fielding: 'Charles Dickens and the Department of Practical Art' (*Modern Language Review*, 48, 3, 1953, pp. 270 - 277)

Michael Slater (ed): *Dickens' Journalism–* vol. 2 *The Amusements of the People 1834 - 51* (Dent , 1997) and vol. 3 *'Gone Astray' and other papers 1851 - 59* (Dent, 1998)

and, of course, Charles Dickens: *Hard Times* (Penguin, 2003, including Dickens's working notes as an appendix)

and *Household Words* 4 December 1852 pp. 265-270

4 On Pugin and Marlborough House, see especially:

Clive Wainwright: 'Principles true and false – Pugin and the foundation of the Museum of Manufactures' (*The Burlington Magazine*, 137, 1994, pp. 357 - 364)

also Rosemary Hill: *God's Architect* (Allen Lane, London 2007, ch 40 'The whole machinery of the clock', pp. 471 - 483)

5 See, in the National Art Library, bound as Parliament Papers/Department of Art/ Report 1, 1852, *The First Report of the Department of Practical Art*

and Department of Science and Art Museum of Ornamental Art – *Catalogue of Examples of False Principles in Decoration*, 1853, pp. 13 - 23

6 On Henry Cole's domestic photographs, see Mark Haworth-Booth: *'Henry Cole as Photographer'* (V&A Album, Autumn 1988, pp. 38 - 45)

7 On Daniel Imhof and the Orchestrion exhibited in 1862, see Q. David Bowers: *Encyclopaedia of Automatic Musical Instruments* (Vestal, New York, 1977, pp. 463 - 479)

8 John Ruskin: *The Two Paths, being lectures on art... delivered in 1858-1859*, Maynard, Merrill, New York, 1893: Lecture 2, 'The Unity of Art' pp. 54 - 57)

9 For more on the relevant history of art and design education, see:

Christopher Frayling: *The Royal College of Art – 150 years of Art and Design* (Barrie & Jenkins, 1987)

Christopher Frayling: *Art and Design, One hundred years of the Royal College of Art* (Collins and Brown, 1999)

Christopher Frayling and Claire Catterall (ed): *Design of the Times – One hundred years of design at the Royal College of Art*, (Richard Dennis/RCA, 1996)